‖‖‖‖‖‖‖‖‖‖‖‖‖‖‖‖
D1360662

LIVE WITH HONOR

TURNING TRAGEDY INTO TRIUMPH

10-26-19

MINERVA,

LIFE IS WHAT YOU MAKE
IT AND ANYTHING IS
POSSIBLE. THANK YOU
FOR BELIEVING IN ME
ALWAYS

MP

1

LIVE WITH HONOR

TURNING TRAGEDY INTO TRIUMPH

MIKE PANUS

10-25-19

MINERVA,

LIFE IS WHAT YOU MAKE IT AND ANYTHING IS POSSIBLE. THANK YOU FOR BELIEVING IN ME ALWAYS

Mike Panus

2019

2

First Printing: 2019

ISBN 978-0-359-77969-7

Mike Panus
PO Box 582
Central Village, CT 06332

Dedication

Bella Marie Panus, you will always be my inspiration and I will continue to show you how it is possible to achieve all you want in life. You push me every day to be the best Dad that I can be. Thank you. This world is better with you in it.

(Charity 5k in Plainfield, CT September 2018)

Contents

Acknowledgements

A VERY SPECIAL THANK YOU: There are many people that have supported me and believed in me from the very beginning when I decided to put my everything into becoming a speaker. Words will never express how grateful I am and the least I can do is mention their names in the closing of my book. Thank you so much: Brian Andstrom, Michael R. Panus, Jane A. Panus, Mario Lang, Erika Lang, Robert Miller, Neal Howe, Carol Howe, Anthony Silvestro, Al Monty, Sue Monty, Heather Either, Mitch Gray, Dave Robbins, Krysten Soldan, Erik McMechen, Dave Schwab, Bryan Stadnicki, Jacquie Burzicki, Jessica Burzycki, Jim Hayes, Harry Thomas, Dave Spurgas, Chris Bahn, Adam Giandomenico.

COVER DESIGN: Samantha Robshaw with Samantha Robshaw Photography took my idea and certainly exceeded all my expectations. When I first saw the cover design, I was speechless and in tears. Thank you so much, Samantha, for knocking this one out of the park.

Eric W. Wright with FSGraphics got the ball rolling with my cover design. He took the time to scan in my Marine Corps photo and do a little bit of photoshopping on my picture. (The picture is from 1999. From being in a frame for so long, the picture was stuck to the glass of the frame, and the color from my dress blues needed a little touching up.) Eric is a great friend, and I cannot thank him enough.

Introduction

First, I would like to talk about my decision of why I became an inspirational and motivational speaker. There have been a few traumatic events that have taken place in my life related to losing my biological mother and the void in my life of just not having unconditional love from her. Never knowing my biological mother and the empty feeling that I have today is part of my inspiration. Keeping her with me in spirit every single day and connecting with people that have lost loved ones is my special gift. As I have gotten older and became a parent myself, I realize how important it is to have that bonding connection with a child and their mother or father.

After I was incarcerated, I began working sales jobs in hopes of finding what I was meant to do. I had one sales job after another and realized I was missing something in my life. The gratification of giving back and making a difference in the world while making a positive impact on people is what fuels me. I believe I was left on this earth for a bigger purpose: to be a speaker and to inspire and motivate people to be the best person they can be every single day.

I have included written testimonials from past speaking engagements and presentations that I've given to military bases, colleges, high schools, and middle schools. I enjoy discussing my firm stance against driving under the influence of alcohol, but also the topics of overcoming adversity, respect for all people regardless of gender, race, financial status, humility, gratitude, and the power to choose happiness every second of your life. My pledge is to honor my friend and my mother every single day as far as I go on in my life and to be an inspiration and a role model to my amazing daughter. In addition, I am committed to showing my daughter and everyone else in the world that you can overcome anything in life and achieve what you want in life, as long as you work as hard as you can to get there.

Please reach out to me to schedule your life-changing event. I would love to be your next speaker at your event – whether it be at a military base, college, high school, middle school, or anywhere with people that are looking to find that message to help them realize how important their life is and how quickly our lives can be turned upside down. Thank you.

FOR MORE INFORMATION: Mike Panus wants to hear from you. For more information about Mike Panus' speaking engagements or to find out how to book Mike for your next event, contact: mike@mikepanus.com 860.334.6222 mikepanus.com

TESTIMONIALS

In April of 2017, Alfa Company was proud to host Mr. Mike Panus as the 2016-2017 Alcohol Awareness Guest Speaker to the Corps of Cadets. Mr. Panus has a tragic story that we all can benefit from. He was just like us saying this will never happen to me... except that it did. His credibility as a Marine veteran resonated with our cadets as he imparted the lessons of experience in a passionate effort to keep others from learning the way he did. His palpable energy and enthusiasm made a good connection as one who has lived the shame of his poor decisions from a single night that forever changed his life. This man is on a vision quest to change the world with his cautionary message balancing positivity with the grim realities of the consequences of his actions of February 5th, 2005 as the black ice combined with his blood alcohol content and the tree around a curve on Route 169 in Lisbon.

His regret is genuine; his remorse compelling; his professional presence redeeming as his authentic message pays tribute to his best friend such that his family's loss will not have been in vain if it can connect and change the behavior of just one person.

Jon Heller
Director, Admiral James M. Loy Institute for Leadership at the U.S. Coast Guard Academy

Our Norwich Free Academy Senior Class of 2019 had the opportunity to have Mike Panus present his life story to us recently. Mike's presentation was powerful and inspiring to our seniors. The students were engrossed in his personal account and engaged actively in his question and answer session at the end.

His message of accepting responsibility and living with integrity was very appropriate to this age group. He spoke from the heart with sensitivity and emotion. He also weaved our school message of "Respect and Responsibility" nicely into the presentation.

I believe we will be making Mike's assembly an annual event for our Senior Class. As one of our students said to me, "That was the best assembly I've ever attended."

Thomas O'Rourke
Bradlaw House Principal, Norwich Free Academy

This past Fall, we had the privilege of having Michael come and share his story with our students. His approach was welcomed and despite the nature of his story, our students listened quite intently. The experience that Michael had endured and the consequences that followed were expressed forthright and never once did he have the "Woe is me" attitude or deflect from any responsibility. Our students were engrossed in his every word and I believe they realized that there were lessons to be learned from Michael's personal tragic issues. His advice on this matter was well received. The impact of his presentation moved many of our students to approach him afterwards with many questions.

Michael's story truly is a powerful lesson for our young people. It's one that teaches the importance of making wise decisions and keeping in mind the consequences that can happen due to poor choices. His honesty and frankness is very compelling.

We're grateful that he came and shared his story with us. It is our sincere hope that other schools will follow suit and invite Michael too. His story is a life changer.

Sincerely,

Patricia Feeney, Principal

Mike Panus' powerful presentation at Griswold High School was an inspiration to our students and staff!

His ability to connect with those around him is incredible! As High School Principal, I find it vital we prepare our students for life after school, inclusive of the impact our decisions have on our future. Mike was able to take very sensitive, and important, personal life experiences and connect with an auditorium full of high school students! This is certainly no easy task. It was amazing to see teenagers sit absolutely silent while completely engaged in every facet of Mike's presentation.

The impact was profound, as evidenced by the line of students that stayed following the presentation to shake Mike's hand, thank him, and make a personal connection to what Mike had shared. It was truly touching to witness! I know this meaningful opportunity helped our students to understand the importance of the choices they make, no matter how big or how small, and the impact those choices have on their lives and the lives of those around them.

Thank you, Mike! You are a true inspiration!

Erin Palonen
Griswold High School, Principal

It is my pleasure to write this testimonial for Michael D. Panus. Griswold High School was fortunate to have Michael at GHS to present his message to our faculty and students in May of 2017.

He has a true story no one will ever forget. A story of going from unbelievable tragedy to motivating, inspiring, and teaching young adults the very real consequences of decision-making. His honest and emotional presentation resonated with the Griswold students and faculty.

I was overwhelmed with his enthusiasm, inspiration, and motivation for life. I highly recommend Michael to any school or educational institution seeking a dynamic and engaging speaker.

Sincerely,

Stephen Cravinho
Campus Wide Athletic and Activities Director, Griswold Public Schools

The word Inspiration comes from the Latin 'Inspirare' or 'to breathe into'. It also comes the Old English meaning to literally to be "In Spirit". From today's vernacular, it simply means to be "mentally stimulated to feel something or do something". And in today's fast-moving world full of its complexities, it seems like we are all looking for some kind of inspiration. To lose weight, find love, improve a relationship, find a better job, or just clean the house after we get the kids off to school. At various times in our lives, we all need someone to encourage us and to lift us up. To let us know that this thing we call 'Life' is a Journey, not a destination. That its constantly evolving and, like our famous New England Weather, sometimes you just have to get through the clouds of today to see the bright blue sky that begins tomorrow anew. The question is: How do you find it? Who can you turn to? The short answer is you find someone you trust. Someone with Integrity. Someone who has been there. Someone who has tasted the bitter pills that Life makes us all swallow but also understands what medicine it takes to get better. Michael is such a person. I have known Michael for many years and, as a management educator myself, I understand full well the need for integrity when speaking. People who have 'been there, done that'. People who know from experience and can relate. Michael is such a person and listening to him speak it is clear that his message not only comes from his experience, but that it comes from his heart. His enthusiasm for life is infectious; his message is inspiring. And when I'm given the privilege of listening to him talk about his life, I always leave the moment mentally stimulated to think better, act better, and to BE better. Listen to him speak. Hear his message. I'm sure you will feel the same way. He is today's kind of Inspiration.

Jim Hayes
Business Owner

I'm writing this letter in recommendation for Mr. Michael Panus, motivational speaker. Mr. Panus came to our school, Ellis Tech, and spoke to our student-athletes in February 2017. Michael brings a very important message to students and people of all ages. The message was that poor decision making can have a huge impact on your entire world around you, and you don't want to live with regrets of poor decision making.

Mr. Panus was very professional in both attire and presentation. His presentation was relevant, as something of this topic always is, but he is relatable to the youth that he speaks to. His personality is one of infectious optimism, which shows a great deal about his character considering all that he has been through. His story is true, and local, having been a student himself in Eastern Connecticut, many students could put themselves in his shoes. Mr. Panus was very responsive to questions from the students and staff and was easy to work with when it came to scheduling his session and fitting it into a busy school schedule.

In today's day where accountability is high, but student entitlement is also very apparent, it is a good message to demonstrate to students that their actions have consequences. He would be a perfect addition to a pre-prom or pre-graduation assembly where his message would directly relate to the theme. I personally hope to have Mr. Panus back at Ellis Tech and I believe your school or organization, if it deals with teenage students, would be fortunate to have Mr. Panus present and speak.

Sincerely,

Brooke DiFormato
Director of Athletics, Ellis Tech

DONNA MARIE PANUS

(Donna Marie Panus on her wedding day to my Dad, Michael R. Panus, 1975)

My biological mother, Donna Marie Panus, passed from this earth at the age of twenty-seven – thirty days after she gave birth to me. Learning about her passing has impacted my life in many ways, but it was not until recently that I realized just how much. One of the most painful parts of not having my mother with me is that I have no idea who she was as a person.

Thankfully, I have people in my life that remember my mom for all she was and all she passed along through her children. The one thing I have heard time and time again is how much she loved being a mother. My older sister Erika was about a year and a half when I was born, so my mom had some time as a mother under her belt before I was born.

I've had the honor to interview both family members and close friends of my mom to learn who she was as a person. She was one of the youngest of six children, and her personality and attitude towards life seem to have shined rather brightly. Hearing how my mom could light up a room just by walking into it and how she could start and maintain a conversation with someone is a personality trait that was passed on to me. She could have a great time no matter where she was. I like to think that if she were alive today, we would be more than mother and son, but friends as well.

One of the better stories told to me talked about my mom's independence. She was a woman that could lay a path wherever she went that would lead to success. I like to think that she passed that along to me as well.

My mom knew how to have a fun time with those around her. Stories about late night parties and Sunday morning coffee dates with her friends allowed me to understand how much she valued time with her friends. Life is what you make of it, and what I am continuing to learn about my mother is that she gave this world and those she knew unconditional love. My mother was not perfect and made mistakes like we all do in life. However, those mistakes and adversity that she faced only made her a better and stronger woman in her short time on this earth.

Every person that I have met who knew my mother has always shared with me that she was always smiling, full of life, and had the best time, no matter what she was doing. These qualities that my mother had are qualities that I try to demonstrate every day and live by.

My mother loved music. Although she loved many groups, the Turtles and Janis Joplin were some of her favorite artists. I know my mother also loved collecting turtles. She even carved a turtle weighing over a hundred pounds out of big rock. My dad still has this carved turtle sitting outside of his house today. I recently had my daughter Bella take a picture with this turtle. Having something like this today that my mom made is very special to me.

I love the thought of my mother and imagining the woman she was while she was on this planet. Many other people that knew my mom like to remember all the great times that they had with her as well. To honor her legacy, I will continue to live my best life possible and make her proud of the only son that she had.

EARLY LIFE

Perseverance and determination were two words often spoken to me as a child. These two words sound simple when read on a piece of paper, but they were engrained into my mind as a child. Hearing "Michael, if you want to succeed you need to be determined and focus on what you want the result to be" was a common occurrence in my childhood.

The expectation to be a leader among men was pressed upon me the moment I entered this world and it has gently pushed me each day since then. The first breath my tiny lungs took in from this world was not a peaceful one, but that of struggle. The world welcomed me with an immediate task the day I was born. The task was to survive knowing that my body was not fully mature. I was to think stronger and act smarter in order to survive both mentally and physically. My tiny lungs inhaled their first breath of this world's air on February 19th, 1980, nearly six weeks premature of my expected arrival date.

Being strong-willed and having a zest for life has always been the way that I have lived my life. This simple, yet significant personality trait has been embedded into my core and because of that, I am here today. My story is unique and the ride until this point has had times as smooth as the water on top of the stillest of ponds before sunrise and as treacherous as a rushing river in the white mountains. I was raised by my father Mike and my stepmother Jane (whom I've always considered to be my mother) in the small town of Plainfield, Connecticut. Growing up in Plainfield was as typical as you may imagine. The community, small and friendly, always had a great reputation and I was proud to be part of it. My family was typical of a middle-class American family – my parents worked extremely hard to give their children the best they could. I am the youngest of three children, yet I am sure I was the most exuberant. Correction, I can absolutely confirm I was the most exuberant of the bunch. My older brother

Rob has the utmost sense of control and calmness, and my sister Erika is America's sweetheart. My siblings and I were all different in our own ways, but our parents loved us all the same. No matter the age, it was expected of all of us to do the "right" thing. Honesty, loyalty, humility, respect, and humbleness were as common as exuding confidence and a willingness to win.

My personality is most definitely a competitive one. I love to win. I love the feeling of accomplishment, and I love to know that my hard work paid off with a positive result. The feeling I got when I made a shot that was nothing but net into the basketball hoop, or when I made a game-saving tackle on the football field, or when I made a game-winning hit on the baseball field sparked my soul. I felt alive, and it fueled my competitive drive. My blood would run through my veins a little harder, my heart would race, and I could feel the bounce in my step that much more while holding my head up even higher. Thankfully, my parents taught my siblings and I how to compete and play with respect and give true sportsmanship to others. Because of these traits, I realized that whether on the field or dealing with adversity in life, we are only as good as the team around us.

Like most young boys, sports were more than a significant part of my life. They were who I was at the time I was playing them. No matter the season, I was consumed with the relevant sport. When asked, "Michael, what is your favorite sport?" my simple reply was "what season are we in?" Football, basketball, baseball, golf, hunting, fishing, you name it – each sport defined me when I was involved with it. My parents knew that if they gave me a ball, club, gun, or pole, I would wear it out quicker than most, and they always had them at the ready. My parents' patience was tested time and time again. I remember working on my baseball swing and using my mom's freshly planted daffodils and tulips as the perfect batting cage targets.

My brother Rob taught me the fundamentals of sports, and he taught me how to compete fairly. Without knowing it, Rob gave me the upper hand when it came to competing against my peers.

By competing with Rob, who was significantly older than I was, I was placed into an environment where I was destined to lose but persevered through to always hold my own. Rob was not only patient and kind, but he was firm and committed to watching me grow and develop into a competitive athlete. One of the greatest things Rob taught me was how to be strong both mentally and physically. I admire Rob for taking the time to teach me and having the patience to guide me. Being the older brother is not always easy. I'm positive I annoyed him at times, but Rob always made me feel like I was of value and let me into his life.

Any time there is an age difference of ten years in siblings, there tends to be an expectation in the way relationships play out. For Rob yes, but for me, no. Perhaps it was the fact that I was the younger sibling and Rob was all I knew. Growing up, my brother was the type of guy to treat me like I was important to him and though differences between Rob and I are great and we aren't even technically blood-related, I always felt accepted by him. Very seldom did I not have my brother next to me on the basketball court or running on a field to catch a football. He was the type of guy that took the time to teach me how to properly catch and how to dribble without tripping over my own feet. Rob and I are not the same type of people as far as our traits, but we always connect on a level that brothers should. Having a ten-year age gap between the two of us brought obstacles throughout our childhood, but somehow, we always found a way to get through them together and become stronger brothers.

One of my fondest memories when I was around the age of seven was when I was invited to go to school with my brother for a day. That morning I got up, so excited to be part of Rob's daily routine. He took the time to help me get ready by making sure my hair was done and my clothes and sneakers were put together nicely. We both waited for the bus, and when it came, I can still remember the sounds of the school bus door opening. I stepped up the stairs and felt the treads under my small feet. I smelled the rubber from the mats and the gas coming from the exhaust. I felt the seats with my small fingers as we walked down the aisle and looked up to make eye contact with the students already seated. The bus was filled with big kids like Rob, and I loved every moment of it. I remember the seat was cold but warmed up after a few moments. Naturally, I got the window seat and as the bus pulled away, I remember the feeling of the cold glass on my nose. I waved goodbye to my house and was off to explore something I never had before.

That bus ride was not easy for my brother. He reminded me while I was writing this book that I managed to climb under the seats as the bus was in motion. But as I walked down the aisle, my brother's peers were taking notice of my charismatic and energetic personality, as well as my deep dimples. Shortly after holding conversations with my new friends, I acquired the nickname "Little Dewey," named after my brother. My experience on the bus that day was much different than Rob's, but nonetheless he reminded me he would do it again in a heartbeat for me.

When I was with Rob, I felt wanted – something I struggled with growing up. Upon arrival to his school, I felt on top of the world walking next to him. My chest was puffed out, and I felt so lucky to be part of a crowd I knew nothing about. I spent the day observing people I wanted to be like. This is something that has stuck with me because I felt Rob's compassion and patience with me that day. Rob could have easily been the big brother that was too old or too cool to interact with someone ten years his junior. He never did that once with me though. Through the years, as I've crossed paths with children, I always think of Rob and how he treated me as a younger brother. I think of what it meant to me to have someone play catch with or learn how to dribble from. I pass that along with most young kids I meet these days, if asked. I've had many instances in life where compassion and patience were needed and because of my brother, I can put these traits into action. If I am out at the park with my daughter and we see a group of young teenagers playing pickup basketball, I tend to ask to take part. I can see the excitement in their eyes knowing that it is time to step their game up to match my athletic abilities, since I am many years senior to them. My brother instilled these values in me, and it is something I will always be grateful for.

When is the earliest time that you can remember as a child? Are those memories great memories or are they traumatic events that seem to be burned into your mind? I have many wonderful memories from my childhood with my brother and sister that make me smile today. I am a parent to Bella Marie Panus, who is currently four years old. Being a parent to Bella has certainly changed my outlook on life. When you are an infant, toddler, kid, teenager, you truly do not know what life is or what our purpose is. When I was growing up, I would have never expected to be where I am today being a published author and an inspiration to so many people.

Basketball was something I played any chance I had. Michael Jordan was my idol and I was convinced that if I drank enough Gatorade, I too, could "be like Mike." There were infinite and creative basketball hoops at my house. Trash cans, sinks, outside garbage baskets, hats, door hanging Nerf basketball hoops, circular laundry baskets, and Rob's long arms making a perfect hoop were just some of the many things I could throw a ball into.

When I was growing up, I remember playing sports outside all the time, no matter what the weather was like or whatever season it was. I remember having a little Fisher Price basketball hoop that had adjustable heights starting out around five feet to maybe as high as seven or eight feet. I played basketball and listened to music in our basement all the time. The basement was filled with dust and leftover tree bark from where my brother and I would haul in wood for the wood stove to heat our home in the colder months. The wood stove gave off so much heat that it felt like I was playing basketball in a dusty dark sauna. I would be a sweaty mess when I was finished. I would pretend that I was Michael Jordan winning the game in the last second, or I would be Larry Bird hitting a last second buzzer beater shot to win the game. I love being competitive in just about anything and everything in life; this was an early characteristic that I remember as a young child. Maybe the reason for this was the fact that I was the youngest of three children in my family and felt like I had to compete in almost every situation growing up. However, I loved every second of it. I did not only play basketball on a plastic adjustable Fisher Price basketball hoop when I was a young child; I had a Boston Celtics backboard basketball hoop that my dad put up on a maple tree at ten feet for my brother and me. I recall many basketball games played on that hoop. It was on a portion of our yard that I wore out until it was a circular shaped packed portion of dirt. We did not have a nice concrete basketball court to play on. Instead, we had packed dirt and grass but I did not care. I loved it and I would play if it was pitch black, freezing cold in the snow, icy, or pouring rain. I also remember getting a new adjustable Graphite Backboard and breakaway rim basketball hoop for Christmas or as a birthday gift. I loved this hoop just like I loved the Fisher Price basketball hoop. I thought I was Michael Jordan making last second winning shots or lowering it down to seven or eight feet and doing the most miraculous dunk that I could imagine.

I also remember playing whiffle ball games in our front yard and playing home run derby as well. I still remember the boundaries of my childhood house and where the foul ground would be; to the left was the road, which was foul, and to the right was the house. In the road the ball was dead, and we would have to look for cars before we went and retrieved the waffle ball, or we could play the ball bouncing off the roof and catch it for an out. Straight away to center field past the couple pine trees that were left from my brother not mowing them over would be a home run. My dad planted little maybe 6-inch-high pine trees to have them grow over the years to give our house some privacy from the busy four-way intersection, but today there is only one remaining and it is nearly thirty feet high.

I was not big into video games when I was growing up as a kid. I did have an Atari, Nintendo, and Sega Genesis, but that was about it. I played mostly sports games and used to love playing NBA Jams and John Madden Football.

I loved music as a kid just as much as I love music today. Every word typed in this book has been typed while I was listening to music some way or another, whether it was on my iPod through headphones or Pandora on my phone. Music has been a release for me to bring my mind to whatever place that I wish. My mom has taught me this by being able to bring your mind's eye to any place that you can imagine. No matter where you are or how difficult your life may be, you can imagine yourself being in the most incredible place if you allow your mind to imagine it.

By this point, I am sure you can see how much of an impact both playing sports and having the bond I do with my family has had on me. Hunting and fishing were no different. My earliest memory involving shooting BB guns was in my backyard. The picnic table, about twenty yards away from my target, was always my sniper position. The corner of the backyard had horseshoe pits, and I used to balance my cans on top of the horseshoe pole. As I would practice my aim, it took patience and discipline to the hold the BB gun as steady as I needed to make an accurate shot. Every time I hit the tin can, I would hear a "tinking" sound that I relate to feeling accomplished and gratified. When I turned twelve, I was able to legally hunt. My dad gave me a Remington 20-gauge shotgun for Christmas. The fact that my dad bought me this was a clear indication that I was maturing, and he trusted me enough to manage my own weapon. After I passed my hunters' safety course, which my sister and I did together, I was ready to put my new shotgun into action.

Pheasant hunting was a regular weekend event tradition in the fall and winter that my Dad and I did together. We often went out on Friday nights stocking the pheasants on the land that we would be hunting before sunrise the next morning. Memories that I hold onto today and the time I spent with my Dad included picking up his friend's Springer Spaniel named Jenny. I remember always being so excited to see Jenny that my dad would let me be the one to take her out of her kennel. Jenny would shake with excitement when she saw us because she knew she was going to be involved in the morning's pheasant hunting trip. Jenny was the pointer that would work the woods like it was her own using her keen sense of scent to lock in on the pheasants' hiding place of safety. Jenny burst with excitement and a sense of accomplishment every time she heard our shotguns fire. This was her time to retrieve the pheasants and bring back the fruits of her labor.

Hunting and fishing were and will always be a way of life in my family. We relied on what we caught and killed for the season to put food on the table. Hunting and fishing gave a relief that there was always a meal in the freezer. My parents worked very hard for everything they had, and they gave us exactly what we needed and not what we always wanted. When hunting, my Dad taught me to take only what is necessary and to respect the land and creatures walking on it. This has translated to me fishing and hunting with proper sportsmanship that I will continue to pass on to my daughter Bella.

The relationship between a father and son develops over time, like anything. Conversations tend to be short and to the point and actions certainly speak louder than words. Hunting gave my dad and I a chance to bond and strengthen our relationship. My dad was always reserved and kept to himself, but when we went hunting, I knew he was relaxed. I could see that for even a few short hours, his daily stresses had lifted from his shoulders. As a child, we take for granted what our parents do for us. Being a parent now, I see how overwhelming life can truly be with the many obstacles we face. The time my dad took to introduce me, teach me, and guide me through something close to him gave me an opportunity to see him in his calm place. I deeply cherish all the silent days sitting patiently waiting for the next deer to come by in the woods while hunting with my dad. The wind would blow through the branches of the trees and the birds would make sounds back and forth to one another. The squirrels would move in a way that made me think a deer was approaching. Often, I was let down to see it was only a squirrel running around looking for its next meal within the leaves. My dad and I would sit in silence, just waiting and listening. Sometimes we would be together, but most times, we would be separated in our own space. To this day, sitting in the woods and having the opportunity to hunt is a fulfilling and therapeutic time that I cherish greatly. I was not able to do this for over eleven years recently, which I will get into more details later.

My mom Jane worked two jobs while furthering her education to complete her bachelor's degree. My dad Mike worked in the local 24 Union as a carpenter. After working a more than eight-hour day, they would come home and be parents to my brother, sister, and me. There was always food on the table, and our clothes were always in line with the latest fashion trends. My mom would go above and beyond to make sure that we fit in with the rest of our peers. My dad would take me to Red Sox games and make sure that I always came home with a pin, pennant, or a baseball. Raising children is no easy task, and if you are a parent, you know what I mean. My parents set the tone for my siblings and me as we all moved on to become parents to our own children. Tough love was present throughout my life, but through tough love there was compassion and understanding. My dad was a provider and took care of us the way he knew best. There was a time in my life when my dad had to take total charge of me as a young adult. He did it with grace, dignity, and a force that showed me he loved me unconditionally. The patience he exuded was admirable, as I know I was a lot to handle as an outgoing, exuberant child. My dad has always put his family first and took charge of any situation involving us.

One of my favorite memories was my family's yearly camping trip to Hopeville Pond State Park in Griswold, Connecticut with the Davis family – my Uncle Don, Aunt Betty-Jo, and my cousins Ashley, Matt, and Nick. Matty, Nick, and I were close in age and this vacation was a time for us to connect. Waking up early in the morning to check our poles to see if we caught a much-anticipated bullhead (catfish) was something I enjoyed each morning as a start to the day. Exploring the campground and spending time with my cousins was something that I enjoyed, even though they were a few years younger than me. Rob had always given me the time when I asked for it, and I did this with my younger cousins. My parents gave us the opportunity to be kids on these trips and enjoy some freedom to explore the campground and interact with others our age. Seeing the world as it is now, I know how grateful I am to have had the opportunity to play outside all day and ride my bike without carrying a cell phone. It was simple for me as a child, yet I understand how complex it was for my parents.

School was not one of my strong suits simply because I loved the social side so much more. I was able to comprehend the information just fine, but talking about what was going on at the playground sparked my interest much more. Keeping my grades above passing level was something I had to do to maintain my place on the sports teams. During elementary school, my desk was often placed at the front of the class near the teacher's desk. I was a distraction to those around me, and it was no surprise that gym class was my favorite and best class. My sister Erika was the complete opposite. She studied hard, always had straight As and ran the nest. She was always someone I tried to be like when it came to education, but my focus was not there. I remember feeling good when I would get a test back with an A, but those times were few and far between. The sense of accomplishment was always a great feeling, and I knew I had what it took. I just needed to find a way to take what was presented to me and learn in a way that I could understand.

As all my classmates were given their superlatives at the eighth-grade end of year commencement, I received the PITA (Pain In The Ass) award. My name was called last and I walked up to the stage with a smile and received it gracefully. As I looked down at the piece of paper, I realized I was the joke at my teachers' expense. I played into it and laughed with everyone, but when I got home from school that afternoon and shared my award with my parents my mom voiced her displeasure. If something like that was presented today, I'm sure it would make the 5:00 evening news, and a lawsuit would be handed to both the town and school. Things were much different back then. Because of my behavior, I lost out on opportunities, such as the eighth-grade class trip to Washington DC. Students earned this trip based on a points system driven by proper behavior. I didn't attend the trip because I didn't accumulate enough points throughout the year. Teachers repeatedly told me I was disruptive, a distraction, and I talked too much. I enjoyed being the center of attention and thrived while talking to people. I was not prescribed medication, given a label, or told I had a problem like so many children are told today. I was often made to feel like I was talking more than listening, but who I am and what I do involves talking. My journey to exude words, thoughts, and positive actions were not going to be hindered by others' opinions. It was no secret that my parents certainly had their work cut out for them with me. Looking back, I see they embraced who I was and gently roped me in when they felt the need.

High school was no different; my passion was surrounding myself with people and being social. My personality provided me the opportunity to have multiple groups of friends. I loved to light up a room when I could see its darkness. The mood of a room changes with one person's positive energy and actions, and I knew this was a gift I had. Whether it was a classroom prepping for a test or a room just filled with stagnant air, I could easily turn the mental venting system on and motivate and inspire all of those around me.

Today, I am confident in who I am as a person. There have been plenty of times in my life where I did not know what to do. But I did know I can take a step back and process whatever obstacle I am facing and decide to take multiple steps forward. Being able to recognize your feelings and emotions before you make an impulsive decision and assessing a situation go hand in hand. I remind my audience of this regularly. When faced with a struggle many of us compromise who we are as a person. We make impulsive decisions or react in a certain way expecting an immediate fix. The number one trait I pride myself on today is living with integrity and never compromising who I am as a man and a person. While growing up, I was faced with considerable adversity. Adversity came on suddenly around the age of seven. I was always confident in the people around me. I thought I knew who played what role in my life until one particular night.

When I was in the first or second grade, my parents explained to Erika and me that our mom Jane was not our biological mother. They explained our biological mother had passed away from cancer thirty days after I was born. That was a night in my life that I will always clearly remember. I was home, and the dog was barking. I heard a knock at the door. Unlike usual, both my parents answered the door. All the specifics of the day were not entirely clear, but I do know a man and a woman walked through the door. My parents greeted them as they would anyone coming to our house. Jackets were taken, and these guests were introduced to Erika and me as we all headed to the dining room table.

"Erika and Michael, these folks are here to take a look at our family and witness that we are who we say we are." My father spoke this sentence in a way that was like any other word he had spoken that day. To me, it seemed as though he just said this without thinking a thing about how he was introducing these strangers to Erika and me.

As an adult, I can only imagine the preparation my father took leading up to this event. The strangers sitting in my home were here to witness my mother and father sign paperwork. My mom Jane was adopting Erika and me, and the signing of two documents made it official on this night.

This was one of the first times in my life, I had no words. There was no more explanation that night around what was happening. The age I was determined the way I thought about this situation.

I absorbed the fact that my mom was not my real mom; I had to question what that meant going forward. If she was not my mom, how could she love me like a mom? How did my real mom die? What happened? What was her name? What was going on?

I went to bed a different person that night. I closed my eyes and awoke the next morning knowing there was only one person I could talk to. Sadness, confusion, loss, emptiness were a few of the emotions that ran through me during this time.

Bill and I met in kindergarten and became best friends immediately. Bill and I had plenty of differences, but our core values always remained the same. Bill and I were two or three years into our friendship when I learned about my biological mother. I remember going into school the morning after I was told I was being adopted and found Bill on the playground and simply said to Bill, "My mom died." Telling Bill this information opened a door for me. I was able to say what I knew and have my best friend hear it before I told other people. If I said this aloud to any adult, they would have thought that my mother Jane had passed away. Panic would have ensued, and I am sure a call home would have been made. Bill took the information and held onto it for me with no immediate response or result. I was able to say what I needed out loud and my best friend Bill absorbed it for me. We went on with our day as we normally do, but deep down we both knew something in my life was going to change. To this day, Bill has been my backbone and our lives have run both parallel and in the same lane depending on where we are both at. The only constant is that no matter where we are, we have each other. Bill is the one friend that knows it all and has accepted me for everything I am. There are no words for Bill that will do him justice. My respect for him runs exactly how it should for a best friend, brother, keeper of trust. To those of you that have such a person in your life, I know you understand this. To those of you that don't, I recommend you open your heart and find one. I would like to say that I have given Bill all he has given to me, but in my humble opinion, I have not.

Donna Marie Panus is my biological mother. My love for her is as great as any child has for their mother, yet I only had thirty days on earth with her, and she was very sick during this time. Our time together was confined within the walls of a hospital. I had no idea she was dying, but she had every idea of how I could live. As a parent we look at our children and imagine all the wonderful things they can accomplish within their life. Did Donna look at me and wish upon me all she didn't accomplish in her life? I stop and think about that often.

She was twenty-seven years old when she passed but lived those years in a way that made an impact on this world. The cancer was found six months into her pregnancy with me. She had not been feeling well and the symptoms were just attributed to being pregnant. It was at the six-month mark that she became very ill and the doctors knew something was wrong. Within a month of finding out she was dying of lung cancer, I was brought into this world prematurely. I was not ready, but the universe had other plans. My mother was not going to survive and the decision to deliver me early was apparent. As I came into this world and took my first breath, it was clear that Donna was taking her last.

No one will ever know what our time together was like except Donna, my mother. Knowing who I am and the father I am to my own daughter leads me to believe that Donna held me with love, respect, kindness, and consideration. Something was instilled in me, and I know she had a part in it. Donna was the first to set the stage for me in this world. I would later come to find out that my personality is a lot like hers. My willingness to motivate came from my mother. Perhaps the brief time I had with her was exactly what I needed to set me on this path. The journey I am on has had many roadblocks and you will read them all. There are times I wish I could hear what she spoke to me while she held me in her arms and replay them.

Donna Marie Panus, I love you and I will carry your spirit and honor you throughout my life. I will live my life to make you proud. This is my promise to you.

LATER YEARS

My path in high school was paved for me by my siblings. Rob had successfully completed each grade and walked away with a diploma. My freshman year was Erika's junior year and her presence on campus was known by all. Erika's reputation was pure gold, so being popular was basically handed to me. She was beautiful, intelligent, driven, focused, and excelled at anything she did. She was class president and held the title seriously. Everyone knew Erika, so by default they automatically knew me. I hung out with multiple groups of friends and was able to get along with just about everyone. When it came to academics, I was not like Erika, but I took the social side as something I was extremely good at. I felt like I was constantly in her shadow and I knew I was not able to achieve half of what she did. Erika and I had common ground in sports, however. Erika was a much more sound athlete than me. She was great in cross country, indoor track, and outdoor track, and I focused on football, golf, indoor track, and skiing.

Looking back on this time, I see that my maturity level was not what it should have been in comparison with many of my peers. Getting good grades was something that did not come easy to me and I never really strived to do better because all I wanted to do was to join the Marines. My response to a bad grade on a test typically resulted in me saying "I'm joining the Marines, so this grade does not matter." It would only be later in life that I would realize the importance of applying myself and studying.

I continued to keep my grades at a level that would allow me to continue to play sports, so I could be involved in the social aspect of being on a team, hanging with my friends, and taking part in events that rallied around sports. I never reached out for extra help when it came to academics. What I can tell you though is that if I stop and focus, I excel at anything I do. I work to teach my audience that putting in the time and effort is something we should all do more of and take pride in everything that you do. I thought joining the Marines would be a simple process, but it was in the Marines that I learned to stop and focus, so I could excel in not only academics, but my everyday life.

I believe that serving this country is one of the greatest things a person can do. From a young age, I just knew that being a Marine was something I could be great at. I would be able to serve in this great country and be part of something way bigger than myself. Understanding that I was going to be part of group of individuals that protected this country kept me focused and motivated to get through high school. My great-grandfather, grandfather, and father all served in the military. To follow in their footsteps was truly an honor. I was determined to become the fourth-generation military in my family.

My parents were behind me in joining the military as soon as possible because I was not disciplined, and I was not as mature as I could have been. Joining the military did and will always turn any boy into a man, and I am living proof of that. I knew it was something I needed. My parents recognized this as well, and because of this, they approved my entrance into the Marines before I turned eighteen. I was seventeen years old the day my parents brought me to the Marine Corps recruiting office one town away in Danielson, Connecticut. After meeting with the recruiter, watching a few videos, and asking a few questions, I was convinced that this was exactly what I wanted to do, and I was ready to go. I was nervous but excited at the same time – nervous about the unknown of serving in the military and what to expect, but excited to see what I would accomplish.

My first recruiter was not what I was hoping for at all. He was very pushy and full of pressure. This was a choice I was making on my own, and I wanted to find the right opportunity for me within the military based off my ASVAB results. ASVAB stands for Armed Services Vocational Aptitude Battery; anyone seeking to join the military must take this test. A high score on this test will improve your chances of getting a specialty job and/or signing bonus. This test is done to see who is qualified to do what and you are matched with jobs based off your skillset. I did well on the ASVAB test and scored higher than most. When I look back on tests and situations I am interested in, I have found that I always achieve a goal. Since this was not the case in high school, I felt a sense of accomplishment and was proud of myself for doing as well as I did on the ASVAB test. Because of my score, I was able to pick from a variety of occupations.

My first choice was in culinary, but after talking to a few people I realized it would not be exactly what I wanted to do. My score allowed me to choose from 80% of the jobs available throughout the military. I wanted to make sure I chose something that not only interested me, but would push me to be the best I could be.

My decision landed in the aviation field, as I thought it would be awesome to have an opportunity to work around aircrafts. My title was Aviation Operations Specialist. As an Aviation Operations Specialist, I was primarily responsible for scheduling and dispatching tactical aircraft missions. I helped operate one of the largest fleet of aircrafts in the world and kept them running safely and efficiently.

When I joined the Marine Corps, I can honestly say that I loved the challenge of being in boot camp. It was challenging in every aspect and pushed me more than I thought. The psychological portion of boot camp was much more mentally challenging than I expected. Drill instructors strategically break you down and form the person they want you to be. There was no more who I wanted to be, simply who they wanted me to be and what the Marine Corps wanted me to be. Until this point in my life, I was my own person. It took honor, courage, commitment, trust, and patience to become part of the Marines and trust that the mentality they were about to instill in me was better than what I could give myself.

Patience was not something I had naturally, but the military certainly taught it to me. Around my junior year in high school I joined the delayed entry program for the military. This is for the people that joined early to prep them for boot camp. I would show up bi-weekly to the recruitment office and the recruiter, along with a few other students would meet for classes. We were challenged with all types of boot camp physical fitness tasks. Running, pushups, pull-ups, jumping-jacks, mountain climbers, and sit-ups were the norm in this class. The goal was to help us get familiarized with what we were to experience in boot camp. We also studied knowledge about the Marine Corps in the classroom, including the General Orders. This was a time to ask questions, familiarize myself with process and procedures, and get ready for boot camp. Towards the end of the delayed entry program, the class and I were sent to Cape Cod, Massachusetts for the weekend for the prep crucible test.

Every Marine must pass what is called a "Crucible Test."[1] This test takes place over fifty-four hours and includes food and sleep deprivation over forty-five miles of marching, combat assault courses, leadership reaction courses, and team-building warrior stations.

I was ready to take this test and prove that I had exactly what was needed for the military. The first day started out as planned, and I was feeling confident, secure, and in control of the tasks ahead of me. However, during one of the exercises, I slipped on a piece of wood suspended in the air by rope attempting to get ammunition boxes across a body of water. When I slipped, I landed directly on the concrete with my left shoulder taking the brunt of the fall. I dislocated my left shoulder, and immediately I was in a lot of pain. I was scared at this point only because if I was truly injured, I would not be able to go any further and my plan to join the Marines would be over. I attempted to hide just how bad the injury was. The excruciating pain that I was feeling was too much and unfortunately, I was not able to go on with the crucible training. There was no way I could hold on to anything.

---

[1] Crucible is a rite of passage that, through shared sacrifice, recruits will never forget. With that memory and the core values learned in recruit training, recruits are able to face any challenges in their path.

My shoulder had been dislocated severely, and the result was that I needed to have surgery quickly. I was held back from all the activities for the remainder of the weekend. I left Cape Cod with the rest of the recruits and returned back home to contact an Orthopedic Specialist.

I was injured and disqualified from being in the Marine Corps for the near future. I was devastated.

Being a Marine was the only thing that I ever wanted, and it was the only thing that I ever knew in life. I was not yet eighteen, but already in a place in my life where I was lost, and I didn't know which direction I was going to go. Fortunately, I had surgery done by a great doctor, and my recovery went extremely well. I attribute my recovery to two things. First, my surgeon was extremely advanced in his profession and knew how to fix my torn rotator cuff. Second, my will to keep on track and become a Marine made me want to recover quickly.

What little patience I had as a teenager was tested, and I had to both focus and understand that with patience I would heal and join the military again. I kept a positive outlook and made a promise to myself that I would keep on my path. I stuck with my physical therapy, communicated clearly to my doctors, voiced my concerns, and became my best advocate. My family helped me with the day to day struggles as I healed, and I made sure to give myself the positive reinforcement that I was in control of my future; I just had to be patient and my time to join the Marines would come. After a shorter recovery than most, but what seemed like a lifetime for me, I was able to have my doctor confirm that I was one-hundred percent healed and able to join back up.

Headquarters of the Marine Corps signed off on me being able to enlist again. I had to re-enlist and did that immediately. I was beyond excited and grateful for the second chance. I was able to start boot camp nine months after I originally planned. Looking back on it now, it does not seem that long, but at the time, it was a true test of my patience. Persistence, determination, and patience all played a key role in achieving this goal.

The night before bootcamp was a night that will always stay with me. My girlfriend spent the night at my parents' house, and we talked about how the next morning would go. At exactly four o'clock in the morning I was dressed and ready to go and saw the headlights of a car pull into the driveway. I said my goodbyes to my Mom, Dad, and girlfriend, and I was out of the door with my recruiter on my way to Springfield, Massachusetts. The MEPS (Military Entrance Processing Command) station was located here, and this is where I would ship out from. I remember feeling a bit nervous, but more excited than anything. From the MEPS station, I would ship to Parris Island since I was on the east side of the Mississippi River. I remember reminding myself that the unknown and unexpected are part of this process. This is something I always struggled with and I had to have trust that the process would guide me.

The drive from my home to Springfield was about an hour and a half and I remember thinking about multiple things. I had just left my family and friends that had been such a big support system in my life; I was turning the page and becoming a man. I was on my way to becoming dependent on only myself and my actions through the process I was about to enter. It was up to me to make it through boot camp and become a Marine. Upon arrival to the MEPS station I prepared my mind one last time and exited the car. All recruits jumped on the bus, and we headed to the airport. I had not flown too many times in my life, so this was also a big thing for me. The flight from Boston to South Carolina was smooth and full of young recruits just like me wondering what the next step would be.

Arriving at the airport in South Carolina was interesting. We were dressed in our civilian clothes, and it seemed like as soon as we exited the plane and entered the airport, there were Drill Instructors waiting for us. The hysteria and orders were immediately taking place. All the recruits loaded onto a bus. The bus ride to Parris Island was relatively short and once the bus stopped, I saw the infamous yellow footprints. These footprints were where you step and start running. Within seconds, your life after that first step changes dramatically because the decisions you made were no longer independent. The second my foot hit the first yellow footprint, I knew I made the right decision. From that point on, I was able to let go of what I wanted to do and let the drill instructors take over. They guided me to become the motivated Marine that I knew I always wanted to become. The next thirteen weeks of my life were full of giving in, putting trust into the process, and allowing the training to take its course.

The physical aspect of boot camp was fun to me because I've always been athletic and active. Running, doing pull ups, and sit ups wasn't as challenging for me as it was for other people that I noticed in my platoon. My platoon number was 1045,1st Battalion Delta Company, and I can still picture it to this day. The barracks were up on the third deck and I could see the swamp, the pit, and parade deck right outside. There were Marines graduating every so often and it was more of a struggle to look at because I had just arrived at boot camp. I had to be patient and knew my time to graduate would come.

When you are part of the military, you do whatever you can to help your peers in any way. I always remember keeping a positive attitude throughout our trainings. I would do my best to help those I saw struggling. I felt confident and was always able to self-motivate. There was no room for failure in my mind, so that attitude was naturally forced out to those around me. By the end of the day, I would try to take a moment to reflect on the accomplishments of the day. These little wins added up in the end and everyone could benefit a little from taking a look at the day's accomplishments.

It is inevitable that not all recruits will pass boot camp. There was no doubt in my mind that I would be one of the few that did successfully complete boot camp. The beginning of boot camp started with nearly ninety recruits but ended with around seventy-five. Most left due to injury, failing the knowledge test, failing the physical fitness test, failing the rifle range, and some even tried taking their own life. Growing up in a family that hunts I was confident in handling a rifle and making precise shots. The only scare I had was on qualification day of the M16 A-2 service rifle. It is imperative that Marines are trained to use an M16 A-2 service rifle. Every Marine needs to be able to take the rifle apart, clean it, and put it back together quickly and efficiently. I remember spending hours and hours on this task to perfect it. This was my tool – just as a carpenter uses their hammer and other necessary tools to build their projects of work – and I had to know every intricate detail of it. This was one of the tools I needed to do my job, but more importantly, I needed this tool to save lives if necessary. The need to learn every little part of that weapon and how to use it to the best of my ability to protect this country was a responsibility I took seriously.

Rifle range training lasted an entire week. The training included leaving my barracks to go to the rifle range barracks. This was completely independent of all other trainings. I was at the rifle range all day learning how to position myself three ways – standing, sitting, and prone. The tasks include firing from all three positions at three different yard lines – the 100-yard line, the 250-yard line, and the 500-yard line. In order to pass training, I had to make a certain number of shots at each yard line. During training I was impressed with my preciseness and ability to make each shot. I had been accustomed to shooting since a young age, so I was confident in the way I handled the rifle.

Qualifying day arrived, and it was a miracle that I passed. To this day, I have no idea what happened. It could have been my nerves getting the best of me or my sight adjustment being a bit off. I passed by one shot, and it was the last shot at the 500yard line that I needed to pass. I needed to hit a bull's eye, and I did it. Failure to hit that bull's eye would have resulted in a delay in graduation, and it was not something I was willing to accept. My dad had been through this training, just as his father and grandfather had.

I was not willing to fail; I remember the letters my dad and I exchanged throughout my time in boot camp. He reminded me constantly that I would achieve my goals. His support was instrumental in my success through this time. My dad served during Vietnam years (1969-1972), which reminded me that having the opportunity to serve this country was a gift not many could handle. Most were hindered by their own internal struggles. I had the mentality and determination to achieve this goal. He reminded me of that often and that is something I am always grateful for. Some of my closest friends are from the Marines, and to this day, I know we have the support of one another. I recently was a groomsman in the wedding of Jorge Martinez, one of my fellow Marines. To this day, my fellow Marines and I still have a tight camaraderie, my dad included.

Graduation day of boot camp arrived, and my family and girlfriend were there to see me graduate. I was extremely proud of my accomplishment and moving to my career in the military. I knew my parents were proud as well, and that made me feel good. After graduation, I was sent to Camp Lejeune in North Carolina for a military combat training, which lasted about a month. It was right around the 4th of July when I arrived, and the weather was very hot and humid. Training consisted of being out in the woods (the "field") for over two weeks at a time. During my time in the field, I worked with multiple types of weapons and learned how to handle a live grenade. The worst part of the training is that you do not have access to showers on a regular basis and the high temperature is accommodating to the chiggers in the area. Pushing through the irritation and pain caused by the chigger bites was a true test of patience and will to not give up. This was a challenging portion of my Marine Corps experience.

(Aviation Operation Specialist School, Meridian, MS, August 1999)

After military combat training, I was sent down to Meridian, Mississippi, where I attended Aviation Operation Specialist school. I remember this school was in a part of the country that was very new to me. It was a thirty-minute cab ride from the airport to the base, which located out in the middle of nowhere in Mississippi. I kind of kept to myself during this time, so I could focus on the next level of Marine Corps. I focused on doing my best each day and was thankful that my career as an Aviation Operation Specialist was underway. The training took four months, and at the end of those four months, my grade point average was number two in the class. This allowed me to have the second pick for duty stations. The number one student with the highest GPA picked to be stationed at the Marine Corps Headquarters in Washington, DC. Since I finished with the second highest GPA, I had the option to choose any other duty station. Places from Arizona, Hawaii, South Carolina, and all over the country were at the tips of my fingers. I looked down the list and I saw that New Orleans, Louisiana, 4th Marine Aircraft Wing was available. My eyes lit up because, about two or three weeks before that, my classmates and I rented a car and spent a few days in New Orleans on an extended sixty-two-hour vacation. I knew I wanted to return and have that as my duty station. I thought it would be a great mix of socialization while serving my country.

(Mardi Gras parade security detail on the Westbank, New Orleans, LA, February 27, 2000)

Across the river from my barracks, I could see the Superdome. I remember hearing the crowd roar when the New Orleans Saints scored a touchdown during a game. It was a sound that was not only comforting, but reminded me to always be the best I could be. I remember serving in New Orleans with Lance Corporal McNeely, a Marine from Tallahassee, Alabama. He was one of my closest friends right from the beginning. We both liked sports, so going out to the French Quarter to watch the Saints games when we could was the norm. He had arrived in New Orleans before me and he was familiar with the area and the popular going out spots. We became close friends and he introduced me to his group of friends. My group grew quickly. and the folks I met along the way all had a significant impact in my life. Sergeant Allan

47

Martens, Corporal Russell Savage, Lance Corporal Brett Powell, Lance Corporal Josh Adair, Sergeant Brice McMinn, and Lance Corporal John Drinankle were a few of my closest friends while I was in New Orleans.

Sergeant Martinez was one of the most influential people in the Marine Corps that I met in New Orleans. He had been in New Orleans a good amount of time before I arrived. He had seen the Marine Corps through a different perspective like myself when it came to study but taught me things I carry with me to this day. I noticed that Sergeant Martinez's uniform was always crisp and tight. This is something I took seriously and wished others had as well. First impressions are critical, and as a Marine, I find it important to always put your best foot forward. My friendship with Sergeant Martinez started from a conversation on how to get our uniforms perfect. Sergeant Martinez was someone that instilled the confidence in me to go to school, attend college, and take part-time classes while I was in the Marines. I always saw him carrying schoolbooks while he was at work in the Marines. He was the one that encouraged me to take a class because the military was paying one hundred percent of our college tuition and books at that time. After four years in the Marine Corps, I knew that the Marine Corps probably wasn't going to be a future career for me. I wanted to better myself and further my education. I was ready to attempt to attend college because before I entered the United States Marine Corps, going to college was such an afterthought.

Almost everyone that I worked around was an officer and normally in the military, you don't really interact much with the officers. There are different levels in the military where you must stay within your pay grade. Being a non-commissioned officer E1, E2, and E3, you normally only interact with those non-commissioned officers. Then when you become a commissioned officer E4, E5, and E6, that is when you interact with that group of Marines. Being in the Aircraft Wing, we worked hand in hand with the pilots, which were part of the O3, O4, O5, and O6 groups.

I took advantage of being around the higher groups and learned all I could.

One of the most respected and most influential Marines that I was lucky to serve under was Colonel Richard Coulter, the Commanding Officer (CO) of the 4th Marine Aircraft Wing. Col Coulter to this day is a great friend that I can call at any time and catch up with what is going on in our lives. Col Coulter was a Marine that everyone gravitated to, and he demonstrated the same amount of respect for every Marine that he served with. His leadership abilities are ones that I have not come across again in my life. Col Coulter and I both enjoyed playing golf, and we both were avid sports fans. These similarities in our lives brought our friendship closer together and the memories serving with him still stick with me today. He has taught me, no matter what your role is in work or life, you should always treat someone the way that you would want to be treated yourself. I am so thankful to Col Coulter for being a big role model in my life.

Also, another staff non-commissioned officer (NCO) that played a big role in my early Marine Corps career was Staff Sergeant Christopher Guthrie. Staff Sergeant Guthrie worked directly with me in 4th Marine Aircraft Wing, and he always took the time to help me grow as a young Marine and young man. He went out of his way to pick me up in my barracks room and drive me to the boat dock every day. We took a little boat and crossed the Mississippi River every day to go to work. I am still good friends with Staff Sergeant Guthrie today and will continue to keep in contact with him.

From the first moment I got to my duty station, I knew I was lucky because normally you have to pay your dues, go through the tough times, and work overnight shifts. I did my fair share, but I think I was given a bit less at times due to the duty station I was in. Even though I was a junior-ranking Marine who served on every extracurricular details (including Color Guard Team, Hurricane Disaster Platoon, retirement ceremonies, the Grand Opening of the WWII museum, Mardi Gras parade security, and many more),

I knew that other Marines in other duty stations did not have the relaxed duty station that I had.

In my opinion, joining the military is one of the most positive things anyone could ever decide to do. I believe it gives you an appreciation for this country and the people that have served before you. We are able to live in a free country because of things like this. I strongly encourage anybody that doesn't have direction in their life and doesn't know where they really want to go to consider joining the military. It gives you an opportunity to not only get out of your current environment and experience seeing parts of the world and the country that you would normally not see, but it also gives you a direction in life. It also gives you a chance to meet some amazing people that will become your brothers and sisters and that you will have life-long friendships with.

When I originally signed up, I did four years active duty and was then obligated to do four years inactive duty. The United States got rid of the draft so anyone serving active duty is required to do inactive duty for a period after. The reason for inactive duty service obligations is to allow the country to bring back inactive military members if we were ever in a time where military members were needed immediately. Instead of drafting people and having them go through long training periods, we could just recall the inactive military members.

My four-year obligation of active duty was up right around the 9/11 attacks, so there was no way I was moving to inactive duty. I was sitting at my desk and was asked to come into an office with CNN on the TV. We were seeing the attacks happen just like the rest of the country. My initial reaction was that some junior pilot had lost control of a private plane. A few moments later, I received a call from my dad asking if I knew what was going on. I had as much information as he did at that time. My sister Erika was working in New York City where some of the attacks were taking place, and my dad was unable to reach her. I heard the panic in his voice. My dad was worried about Erika and he felt that I would maybe know something he wouldn't.

I was assigned to twenty-four-hour security duty at the base. Our country was under attack and anything could happen at any moment. New Orleans is one of the biggest ports in the US with the Mississippi River being the in and out of the area. We would see hundreds of barge ships moving up and down the Mississippi River, and a lot of goods are transported from the Gulf of Mexico all the way up to Canada. This was an area that we thought could have been next for attacks. I can assure you that even though I willingly chose to serve this country, I still had a bit of panic knowing we were under attack. My skills and education to this point were put to the test. I was taught in boot camp and the Marines that no matter what it is that you are dealt with that you were given the confidence to take on any obstacle put in front of you. Any time I am faced with an obstacle, my Marine "instinct" kicks in. You are trusted to do a job just like everyone else is trusted to do a job. Whatever it is that you do for a profession, do the job to the best of your ability. As a Marine, no matter what happens and whether it's during wartime or peacetime you trust in what you were taught and do the next right thing.

The Marine Corps instills confidence in you from very early on in boot camp; you continuously master every activity from the second you step foot on those infamous yellow footprints. That's one of the earliest things that's instilled in you. They break you down and make you realize that what you were before is not what you will come out to be. You are molded into the strong confident Marine that you will continue to be even after serving this great country. The core values that are instilled in you as a Marine during boot camp are values that will stick with you for life – honor, courage, and commitment. After the confidence is instilled in the young Marines, they realize that no task or goal is unattainable. It becomes a matter of determination and perseverance and a positive mindset. Thanks to the Marines, I had the confidence to further my education and attend college.

I did very well in the college courses that I started to take while I was serving in the Marine Corps. I remember one of the first classes that I took was essentials of writing. I got an A in that class. I called home to inform my parents that I not only passed the class but got an A. I told my mom and dad that I was smart enough for college, which in the past I had never thought was true. It took getting through four years of the Marine Corps to understand that being disciplined and confident in my studies was all I needed. I was able to enroll at a local community college called Delgado Community College while still on active duty. I finally felt like this was going to change my life for the better. I anticipated getting out of the Marines in March of 2003, so I enrolled in a full course load of classes at the community college. My girlfriend at the time was from New Orleans so I planned to stay in the area and had no plans to move back to Connecticut anytime soon. However because of the terrorist attacks on 9/11 and the stop-loss taking place, I wasn't able to get out of the Marine Corps when I was originally scheduled to and become a civilian. My Colonel at the time allowed me to continue to go to college, while I was still serving as an active duty Marine because I had already enrolled in a full semester of classes. I remember going to school in the morning and being able to come back after lunch, put my Marine Corps uniform on, and perform the job the Marines required me to do.

I was very fortunate and lucky that I was able to keep attending college and further my education. Having a full load of courses and continue to serve this country was not easy, but I was focused and determined. I ended up receiving my Associate's degree from the local community college.

After graduation, I ended up driving across the country with Dave Schwab, a very close friend of mine, to return home to see my friends and family that I had missed over the four and a half years that I was away. I think that was the biggest reason why I decided to leave New Orleans – I missed my friends and my family and wanted to be back with them to continue to further my education in college. I had my transcript sent home from Delgado Community College and all my credits transferred over at the University where I decide to attend. I was set to study business administration with a minor in marketing at Eastern Connecticut State University. The 4.0 GPA I had through my time in New Orleans was left in New Orleans. I was proud to say that I had a 4.0 on that transcript, but I had to start from scratch with my next sixty credits at my new university. When I started to take my upper level classes in college, it was a little harder than my previous college classes. I looked at it optimistically and did well even though they were tougher classes.

Since I served my country and joined the Marine Corps right after high school, I felt like I always needed to catch up to my peers that left right after high school to go to college and start their careers and move forward in their life. I took advantage of every opportunity and took as many courses as I could per semester. I took courses during breaks as well, just to move through as quickly as possible. I was always in a rush and I was always on the go, so taking as many courses as I could felt normal. Fortunately, my parents always offered a roof for me to stay under and didn't ask for rent. I did want to have some money to go out and have fun, so I took a valet parking job at a local casino. I hustled more than the average valet attendant. The casino was full of cash, and I wanted an opportunity to make as much money as I could. Most would say that they didn't like my work ethic, because I hustled a lot and I was able to make more money than them. I had just left the Marine Corps where I worked my ass off under extremely strenuous circumstances, so working as a valet attendant was like being at a playground. The folks around me were not accustomed to the work ethic I had. It didn't matter if I was parking cars or defending this country, I did my job and I did it well. I always give everything that I am doing everything that I have.

The one person I did hit it off with was the doorman that I talked to each time I worked. At first, we didn't hit it off, but after a while he took a liking to me. About a few months into my time as a valet attendant, my friend the doorman asked if I ever thought about being a bartender. The closest thing I knew about being a bartender was based off the movie Cocktail. I told him I thought the movie was good, so I could consider myself being a bartender. I thought with my friendly and outgoing personality, it would be a perfect job opportunity for me. How hard could it be? Surprisingly, he was serious. He told me he thought I could make a killing because of my personality and told me his brother was the Club Steward over at a local yacht club. My friend told me that if I took the Connecticut certification class to become a bartender, he would let his brother know that he should hire me.

Sure enough, I took a one weekend certification class and showed up to the yacht club the following Friday. I met with the Club Steward, and as promised I walked out of the first interview with my first bartending gig that night. Hindsight is twenty-twenty, and I probably should have eased into my bartending career, but they offered me the opportunity to work a large wedding that night. I knew the money would be huge, so I took it. I was able to pick up jobs that were for people with a good social presence. They were not permanent positions, but they were fun and let me socialize – something that I have always loved to do.

I remember being in college and seeing some students that lived on campus come to class in what seemed like a comatose state. Most would roll out of bed and get to class whenever they felt like or didn't seem too motivated while they were in class. I was the complete opposite and was always on time to class, even though I commuted to school about forty-five minutes away. I took pride in never missing a class while I was in college. Every single class that was scheduled I attended. I had a perfect attendance all through college, and I took pride in that. That's almost unheard of for most college students. It's the norm to skip a class here or there, but I took pride in showing up to every class and doing the best I could. It paid off because I was up to a 3.4 GPA in college and was inducted into the national leadership honor society,

Omicron Delta Kappa, because of the leadership that I had shown in all my classes.

One of my favorite business classes was where I met a great group of friends that I am still very close with today. We were all driven and motivated to pass the course with As. We studied together and motivated each other to be the best we could be. Two of my buddies lived on campus, so I was able to experience the on-campus living experience a little bit as well. It was a perfect balance. Sean, a friend that I met as soon as I started attending Eastern Connecticut State University, became my closest friend. We had our weekly routine. We would always get lunch on Thursdays after class and then hang out at Sean's apartment. This was our regular place to watch sports games or go out and have some fun like any normal college kid would. Balancing work and play was never a hard thing for me. I always knew when it was time to be disciplined and study and when it was ok to take a break. I would get my homework done, prepare presentations, and study for exams just as easily as I could go out and hang with friends for the night. I always found the time to put school first and then find the time to enjoy myself after a stressful week of classes, presentations, and exams. I was able to go out and enjoy the social and partying aspect of college and having fun with my friends. I remember I was in the computer lab always working on presentations and projects and getting things accomplished. My good friends from my business class and I would all meet there to work on the course material. We were a great group of friends and relied on one another to help as needed. I felt like I had a good balance to my life. I was excelling in school, working a job that allowed me to be social, making decent money, and had a group of friends I knew I could rely on.

My good friend Lisa always aced every single exam, quiz, and presentation. She had one of the most positive, upbeat, and outgoing personalities I had ever met. Lisa and I pretty much clicked and became great friends right from the first week of class. I immediately realized how smart and motivated she was. I was proud to call her a friend then, and I am still honored to be her friend today. I was envious of her work ethic and how well she did in college, and I strived to get to that level as well. Lisa reminded me of my sister who always did very well in school and overachieved in all she did. Lisa and I had a very similar personalities and I admired that. Lisa and I were both inducted into the National Leadership Honor Society together. Lisa recently gave up some of her time in her busy life as a mother of two children, a wife to a great husband, and six months pregnant to their third child to come see me speak at her alma mater high school, North Branford High School. For her to take the time to come see me speak means more to me than words could ever express.

I was driven to the point where I was making the Dean's List almost every semester, the complete opposite of high school. Seeing my name on the list motivated me and confirmed I was making all the right choices in my life to better myself. The military had given me the confidence to attend college, and I had the focus to excel now. At this point being disciplined and working hard in college was allowing me to realize that I could achieve great things. In addition, the group of friends that I had met in college were pushing me to be the best I could be.

Winter break was starting, and I was entering my last semester of college. I was taking eighteen credits, and as you go further into college, the classes are higher level and require a lot more work and projects compared to lower level classes. Having eighteen hours in my last semester in the highest level of college courses was challenging, so I was thankful that all I had to do is graduate. Like everyone else, I remember going back to school and like normal, I was in the computer lab with my group of friends getting ready to finish this chapter in my life. The feelings got overwhelming at times because I was not sure how I was going to manage the courses; they were tough in addition to working part-time as a bartender. The week after returning from break I was scheduled to work the weekend at the yacht club, Saturday and

Super Bowl Sunday. I finished school for the week on Thursday and had Friday off. I was ready to go out and let loose and enjoy an evening out with my friends, work the weekend, and head back to class Monday morning.

However, my friends at school and my professors did not see me attend classes that Monday. I was always on time and very punctual for every class. The reason I was absent from class on Monday was due to an event that would ultimately change my life and many other lives forever.

A NIGHT THAT I WOULD DO ANYTHING TO TAKE BACK

(My 2001 Nissan Maxima after the tragic accident. I was ejected from the opening where my door popped open. I struck the tree on the driver's side backseat.)

I was beyond excited to start my last semester of school at Eastern Connecticut State University. Less than ten years earlier, I had one mission in mind – going into the Marine Corps. I was now getting ready to graduate college, something I never thought was possible. My grades were above average, I was doing very well with 3.4 GPA, and I had recently been inducted into the National Leadership Honors Society. I was ecstatic that I would be graduating from college soon and I was going to enjoy the last semester and work very hard, but still find the time to go out and have fun with my friends.

It was a Friday and I didn't have any classes on that day. I spent the previous night at my friend's apartment after going out with my friends on Thursday evening. It snowed four or five inches that evening, a typical February winter day in Connecticut. I woke up to the sun shining, so I left my friend's apartment on campus at Eastern Connecticut State University and went about my day completing some errands. I went up to the Navy Federal Bank on base in Groton, Connecticut to pay my car bill and came home back into town. I got my haircut and worked out at my regular gym.

It was there that I saw my good friend Rich Bronson. The two of us struck up a conversation as normal and chatted a bit about our weekend plans. I mentioned to Rich that I was going to go up to The University of Connecticut to a bar that I would regularly go to with my friends. He asked if he could join us. I was overly excited because Rich and I had talked about going out multiple times, but we had never found times in our busy schedules to go out together. When I finished up at the gym, Rich and I discussed when we would meet up to head out for the night.

In total, there would be five of us going out that night. I went home, showered, and got ready to go out. As I was leaving the house, my mom had mentioned to me that the temperature might drop later and to be careful on the roads. I remember hearing my mom tell me about black ice. I responded that I heard her and said, "No problem Mom, I will see you tomorrow" as I walked out the door. With my freshly ironed shirt in hand, I walked out the door and was on my way to have a fun night with my friends.

I hung my shirt up in the backseat of my car like I had always done figuring I would put it on right before I got to the bar. I'm the type of person that likes a crisp shirt always. I went up the road, stopped at a liquor store, and picked up a six pack of beer and told Rich I was going to meet him at his friend's house that was having a birthday party. I arrived at the birthday party, interacted with everyone, and enjoyed a beer before Rich and I headed out.

On our way out, I remember going next door to check out the neighbor's house as he was a big hunter. He had some stuffed animals on his wall that he had hunted, and I wanted to go see them. On our way to the neighbor's house, I remember feeling how cold it was. As we stepped on the back deck one of our friends took a pretty nasty fall due to the ice that had frozen on the deck. Rich and I left the birthday party, and I followed him to his parent's house. He dropped off his car and jumped in the car with me. Before we started the night, we picked up two of our other friends on our way up to UCONN. The night started like any other typical Friday night out with our friends. I remember we pulled up to the parking area of the bar, which is on the campus at the University of Connecticut. My friends got out of my car and quickly went inside while I put on the button up shirt that I had ironed and had hanging up in the backseat of my car. The shirt was not the original one I chose, but one that a friend had let me borrow because I saw it at his house and I liked it better than the one I previously brought. I hurried up, stood outside, buttoned up my buttons on my shirt, and ran into the bar.

The music was playing, and we all ordered drinks. The night was relaxing, fun, and full of energy. The bar was packed and as a single guy in college, I just loved being out interacting with other people, dancing, and meeting new people. I met a new friend at the bar that evening, and I promised her that I would bring her home safely. When the bar closed at two a.m., my friends and I jumped in my car to drop off my new friend on campus and then went to the closest convenience store to grab a little snack on the way home. I took the regular route home. On my way I dropped off one friend at Eastern Connecticut State University and then next, my friend who lived on my way home. I had borrowed a shirt from this friend earlier in the evening, so I ran into the house to return it back and grab my initial shirt that I had brought. When I got back to the car, Rich, who was originally in the back seat, had moved to the front.

Rich and I were about fifteen minutes from home. His parents lived just about two miles from my parents, so the drive was quick. I was driving the regular route home, but it was dark and cold out. I was aware of my surroundings and not driving over the speed limit. I came down and around a hill that I had done many times before and was getting ready to turn a corner that was familiar to me. My car went over a patch of black ice and started to slide off the road. I overcompensated my car, slid off the road, and struck a tree that was directly right on the side of the road.

My car struck the tree right behind the driver's side of my 2001 Nissan Maxima. I was ejected nearly twenty feet from the vehicle, because I was not wearing my seatbelt. The time after I struck the tree can be remembered only by the ones that came to rescue us. I was ejected from my car and was laying in the fetal position in the snow for approximately twenty-five minutes.

A young man driving on the same road noticed my car crashed up on the side of the road up against the tree. He parked his truck across the street from my vehicle. He attempted to cross the street to see what was going on and call 911, but while crossing the street, he slipped two times because the road was so icy. He first saw me laying in the front yard of someone's house in the fetal position. He called 911 and went over to the other side of the vehicle. It was then he saw my friend Rich hunched over in the front seat of my car.

Rich was pronounced dead on the scene of the accident. He did not have a heartbeat or a pulse. I was rushed to a local hospital and brought in through the emergency room. I had suffered a traumatic brain injury, three broken ribs, a punctured lung, broken shoulder, and a broken hand. I was in a coma for four days. The breathing machine and IVs were the only things keeping me alive.

Everything around this time of my life is a blur because I had a traumatic brain injury. I don't remember much from the hospital. I do remember having my friends and family there after I woke up from the coma. They told me my friend Rich had passed away in the accident that I caused by drinking and driving. I was really lost at that point; I fully didn't really understand what was happening. The doctors and my family had told me that my friend had passed away, but minutes after I would say, "I hope Rich is doing better than I am."

I have very few memories about the night of the accident. I remember it being cold and I remember I was out to have a fun night out with my friends. I wanted to make sure Rich had an awesome time. It was our first time that we'd ever gone out together, so I was happy to drive for my friends. Everything I can tell you from the night is due to what was written on the police report and in my medical records and what has been told to me by my friends and family. The basics such as stopping by the convenience store to grab a snack and getting out of the car to return a shirt to my friend are clear in my mind, but everything else was lost the moment I slid on the ice. I do remember leaving my friend's house. Rich had fallen asleep in the back seat but moved to the front since he and I were the only two left in the car. We were approximately fifteen minutes from our houses. I remember coming down Gooseneck Hill Road, which was less than five minutes before the accident happened. The road was slippery, and I remember slowing my speed to accommodate the weather. Down the road a few minutes later is where I struck the patch of black ice and crashed my car.

My time in the hospital was a blur as well. I was in a coma for four days and when I awoke, I had short term memory loss. The hospital suggested that I go to a rehabilitation center for a week or so, but my parents and I told the hospital that I would be just fine going home. My parents would take care of me, and we all thought it was best if I just was back in an environment that was comfortable for me. I could rest easy and not have as much panic about who was going to walk through the door.

Because of the injuries sustained, I had to sleep on the couch. My room was upstairs and there was no way I could climb stairs at that point. The brain injury, broken ribs, compound fracture in my hand, and broken shoulder stopped me from being mobile. Neither myself nor my parents were willing to take the risk of me falling down the stairs and causing more injuries. My mom spent a lot of time with me in the living room. We would watch movies and she would stay close while I rested. I remember asking my Mom "Why me? Why was I left here, and Rich was taken?" This accident was something that I never ever intended to happen, and the pain I caused was too much to bear at times.

Being a strong-minded person that I've always been and knowing how to fight and survive allowed me to gain the strength to keep fighting. I knew there were bigger things in my life that I would do one day, and I almost immediately knew that I was going to give back and speak to other people about not causing the same type of tragedy that I did. However, it would not be until a little bit later in life. At this point, I just was getting the physical injuries taken care of. Physical therapy helped for the compound fracture my hand sustained. I had an allergic reaction to a medicine that I was given and got so sick that I could not stop vomiting. The pain that ensued from vomiting with three broken ribs is something that can't be put into words. I remember trying to hold my ribs tightly, so they would not break more than they already were.

I had a chipped tooth and I didn't even realize this until I came home from the hospital and had a sip of water and felt the pain from the exposed nerve in my chipped tooth. I had been on pain medication in the hospital, but when I was home, I tried staying away from it as much as I could. A sip of water caused the nerves in my tooth to be touched and it was an unexpected pain. I had to get that repaired shortly after the accident.

Physical therapy helped not only my hand and shoulder, but also my brain. I had to relearn to think and talk properly. I realized immediately how much my brain injury impacted me because while watching movies I had watched many times in the past, I could not remember actors' names. This really bothered me. I remember watching Top Gun and having no clue who Tom Cruise was. Today, I have a good memory and can function like I normally did, but not knowing if I would ever fully recover was something that bothered me.

I told my Mom that I was so sorry and remorseful for everything that I caused and was going to go out and speak to people. I remember sharing that with her very early on. I felt not only an obligation, but that it was truly something I had to do, more like my purpose in life now. I had to drop my classes for that last semester of college because I was in the hospital and then home recovering. Missing two weeks took me out of the semester, so I had to wait for the next semester to go back. I was accustomed to taking fifteen or eighteen hours each semester, but because of my brain injury, I was only able to take twelve hours or four classes. With my expectation of finishing as soon as possible, I was upset that I had to now go through two more semesters. I did continue to take courses as a full-time student, so I would be eligible for the G.I Bill. My brain wasn't the same because the material that came easy in the past was something I could no longer retain. I got a C on my first quiz after returning to school after the accident. I never really got C's ever in college, and it was more difficult for me to retain the information. I knew I had to study harder and that's what I did. I realized that I had an injury and I needed to overcome it.

I pushed a little harder and did a little more work than I normally did in the past and kept my grade point average at a place above average. The stress of the accident, the loss of my friend, and school was noticeable, so I decided to take a vacation to San Diego before I started my next winter session. A couple of my friends and I decided to go enjoy the weather. My cousin Cliff lived out there at the time, so we had a place to stay. That was where I had met a girl named Stephanie.

My friends and I had been out one night, and Stephanie and her friend were at the same club. Out of all the women that I had seen that evening, I noticed her from across the room and excitedly approached her. We danced and hit it off, so numbers were exchanged at the end of the night. We also brought her and her friend home. Stephanie and I met for lunch the next day and I found out she was a traveling nurse from Indiana. The weekend that I had met Stephanie was her last weekend in San Diego before she started a new assignment in San Francisco. Stephanie and I certainly felt an immediate connection.

I flew back home to Connecticut, but we kept in touch with each other. California to Connecticut has a three-hour difference, so it was difficult for me to stay up late most nights to connect but we did, and the two of us fell in love. I was in one of the toughest times of my life, and Stephanie was there for me and truly opened her heart to me. I traveled out to see her in San Francisco during my spring break. We had an amazing time sightseeing and being part of each other's life. I remember being so excited to spend a week with her and every single second of my trip was incredible. Stephanie and I had only spent probably less than three hours together from dancing at the club when I first met her and then lunch the next day. I knew that I could not wait to see Stephanie and spend more time with her, so that is why I was confident in me booking a trip across the country to be with her would be nothing short of amazing. Managing to stay in touch with a three-hour time difference and trusting one another with great communication left me to believe that my instincts would be correct. Stephanie was able to take an assignment in Boston and we planned on moving in together in Boston after she was finished with her assignment in San Francisco. She would be working at a children's hospital in Boston and currently I was getting ready to graduate college. I flew out to San Francisco, CA and we drove together to Indiana to her parents' house. I flew back to Connecticut, took my finals for my last semester, and then flew back to Indiana. We then made a trip from Indiana to Massachusetts. We arrived back to Massachusetts on May 5, 2006 (Cinco de Mayo). Stephanie and I drove to Bill Jolley my best friend's house, and he and his wife Lindsey made dinner for the four of us. We spent the night there and then moved into Stephanie's apartment in Beacon Hill, Boston the next day.

I was just about ready to graduate college and continued working at the Westerly Yacht Club as a bartender. I would go from Boston to Westerly, RI to work a couple of shifts a week but decided that a job in Boston would be better. Luckily, we were not far from Newbury Street, so I landed a job as a server at an upscale, busy restaurant, and coincidentally the name of the restaurant was Stephanie's on Newbury Street.

I was back and forth with court at the time as well, so my stress levels were high. I had been arrested for second degree manslaughter with a motor vehicle under the influence of alcohol which was a felony, facing up to ten and a half years in prison. I was lost. Mentally, I had no idea what was going to happen.

I knew Rich's family was very upset, hurt, devastated, and I was responsible for all of it. They didn't want to talk to me at all. All I wanted to do was tell them how sorry I was, but I didn't have that opportunity.

We continued to go to court and I continued to work up in Boston making pretty good money. I enjoyed time with my girlfriend Stephanie, and she was supportive through the entire process. She came to court with me each time. My final court appearance left me with the judge saying that if I plead guilty, I would get five years. If I did not plead guilty, it was going to go to a full-blown jury trial. My attorney said to the judge, "This is a Marine and a college graduate who has never been arrested and has a clean record. What is five years in prison going to do good for this man?"

My family, my attorney, and I decided to go to a full-blown jury trial and not take the only offer of a five-year prison sentence. No matter how long of a prison sentence that I was going to serve, it would never change or erase the pain that I have caused. I spent a few more weeks with Stephanie and decided I was going to move back home in with my parents to prepare for the trial. Stephanie had decided to go back to California when the trial started.

I was afraid to go out and be seen in public in my local community because of what I had caused. Something that bothered me greatly was that initially I was afraid to go to the gym like I once had in the past – the same gym where Rich and I would always see one another and where our friendship began to flourish. Once I was able to go, I was afraid to see anyone. I was the exact opposite of how I had been in the past. I was always outgoing, friendly and cracked a joke with everyone I met. Now, I was always looking over my shoulder and scared of what people thought about me and what I caused. I still carry this with me at times today.

THE TRIAL

Each day of the trial was the same for the most part in terms of schedule, but the information provided was a reminder of what pain I caused Rich's family. Each day was a new feeling of pain, regret, shame, guilt, and uncertainty. Facing the unknown and the real possibility of ten plus years in prison didn't scare me. Being convicted and being found guilty by a jury was not what bothered me. What bothered me was that I was not able to take back my poor decision and give Rich back his life. The hell I was living in was minimal to the pain I knew I caused Rich's family. Looking at Rich's parents Mr. and Mrs. Bronson in the courtroom was the hardest part of this all. I wanted nothing more than to have them feel how sorry I truly was and still am.

On February 5, 2005, I made a terrible and selfish decision. I intended it to be a normal night out to celebrate with my friends. However, it resulted in an unthinkable tragedy and that is something that is with me every single day, every single night, every single second of my life. The moment I woke up from the coma and realized what I caused, my lingering pain has been tattooed on my mind and heart. To some, me saying I carry this on my heart means that I may someday be able to accept it and move on. However, this is never going to happen. I won't allow it to leave me because I will never forget my friend Rich and I will continue to honor him and carry on his legacy.

I stand in front of hundreds, sometimes thousands of people, and pour my heart out in hopes that I can educate just one person in the real possibility that they could be in my shoes. I wish this upon no one. Every day, I think about what I would do differently and if I could take back that selfish choice that I made that early morning on February 5, 2005.

My attorney suggested we take this to trial because, as I mentioned before, I was not someone with a record or someone who had so much as a run in with the law. I was a Marine who believed in doing right by myself and others around me.

The day we decided to go to trial, I remember walking outside the court and feeling my knees buckle. I cried and felt that the unknown would be the only thing that I knew at that time. I was emotionally drained and didn't know what to do. I didn't know what to expect. All I wanted to do was to say how sorry I was to Rich's parents and move forward in my life and make a difference in other people's lives. However, I knew that was not a possibility.

Reliving the night of the accident through the trial put stress on everyone. I could see the stress on the faces of everyone involved. I felt the stress in my own body, and when I looked in the mirror, I saw it on my face. Hearing the testimonies from my friends, seeing the toxicologist reports, the reports from the State police, and the testimony from the EMTs will stay in my mind forever. Also, the demeanor and looks on all of my family and friends' faces and body will be ingrained in my mind forever. I truly will never be able to find the words to tell all my family and friends how grateful I am for all of their support during that time. Sitting in that courtroom daily for about a month took the life out of everyone in there. The courtroom was full of people I knew. Both Rich's family and my family and friends came to watch, listen, and ultimately come to their own personal conclusions. This was a perfect example of an emotional rollercoaster.

The trial ended, and the jury was in deliberations for a few days. The jury deliberations took what seemed to be forever. Later I would learn what happened behind those doors during deliberations. During that time, I was like a leaf floating in the air getting blown around by the wind. The wind was too strong for me, and I had to go with whatever direction it chose to go. My entire life up to that point was defined by living a life that I had control of and being the best I could be. During the trial and jury deliberations, I had no control of what was going to happen, and I had to accept it. Acceptance would become something I would get good at over the years. I would learn to take responsibility of a situation and do the best I could.

It was a Tuesday afternoon, and we all came back to the courthouse from lunch like normal. The jury was not finished with deliberations, so I went outside to get some fresh air. I took a walk down by the river near the courthouse with my Uncle Dom. My cell phone rang in my pocket, and it was my mom calling to tell me that the jury had decided a verdict. When your gut tells you something, it is best to listen to it. I knew immediately what was going to happen, I could feel it. I would be going to jail.

I never once felt sorry for myself. Instead, I felt whatever the jury handed me, I would accept. I needed to accept it to help Rich's family gain a little closure. I was determined to use this time to start the process of healing, forgiveness, and acceptance.

I returned to the courtroom and stood with my head held high and my back straight as the jury read the verdict. I was found guilty of second-degree manslaughter with a motor vehicle under the influence of alcohol. I took the chain with a cross off my neck and handed it to my mom. I then took my suit jacket off and handed it to both my mom and dad. I was able to give them a hug good-bye before the state marshal escorted me away. I still remember to this day what color button-up shirt I was wearing (baby blue) and the tie that I had on (a blue tie with off white tulips) – a tie that my Mom had bought for me when we were in Germany. The scene was emotional. No one in the courtroom seemed pleased; there were no winners or losers. Rich's parents had gained a bit of closure, but I knew we all had a long road of healing ahead of us.

Everyone would have to heal in their own way. I walked away and from that moment on, I took full responsibility of my actions but held onto what I knew was true. A jury found me guilty of my actions, but it would not shape me as a person or change how I thought or how I felt about anything. I knew I was the one that I made a terrible mistake and a selfish decision.

I was originally charged with negligent homicide with a motor vehicle, which was a misdemeanor, facing up to one year in prison. The original charge was changed to a felony, and I was ultimately charged with second degree manslaughter with a motor vehicle under the influence of alcohol. I was sentenced to five and a half years in prison followed by five years' probation.

From the moment I stepped behind the prison walls, I was determined to live my life in the most positive way possible. I knew I was going to make an impact on people's lives in a positive way. I could have easily decided to give up and have a "poor me" attitude. However, from the day I stepped into prison, I remained positive, optimistic, determined, and motivated, knowing that one day I would have a great life. Every single day I spent in prison I reminded myself it was one day closer to having the life that I knew I was left here to have.

Rich was not able to move on in his life. I would do anything in my power to take back that decision and make sure that we all made it home safely that night. However, I cannot erase history. I cannot take back the selfish decision that I made that night. The way I have handled myself throughout this journey has been to always take responsibility. While being incarcerated my mindset was something I could control and use to make a positive impact on others. I helped others that were incarcerated by tutoring them, so they could obtain a GED. I took the opportunities placed in front of me to help in any way that I could. I would serve the correctional officers in the break room and clean it. I tutored the college courses that were offered to the inmates. I became an outside clearance inmate that was able to be trusted outside of prison grounds. I would rake leaves, shovel snow, pick up sticks, paint garbage dumpsters, and be grateful while doing it. I was thankful for breathing the fresh air outside of that prison and being able to help, mentor, and tutor my fellow inmates.

LIFE IN PRISON

It was May 1, 2007, and I was found guilty of 2nd Degree Manslaughter with a motor vehicle while under the influence of alcohol and driving under the influence of alcohol.

I took off my necklace with a cross on it, took off my suit jacket, and gave my dad and mom a hug goodbye. I was then escorted away by the state marshals and brought down to a prison cell. This cell was considered a holding cell until it was time to round up all the inmates to bring them back to prison.

I remember the marshals felt bad for me, so they moved me to a holding cell all by myself. Mentally drained and exhausted, I sat down on the bench in the cell and then laid on my back and closed my eyes. Before I was found guilty, my parents and I had spoken about what would happen if I was found guilty. When you are first found guilty you have two choices. The first choice is to be bailed out for a few weeks before you have to turn yourself in and begin serving whatever you get sentenced to. The second choice is to start serving prison time immediately. My family and I decided since I wanted to get the sentence over as quickly as possible that I would start serving my sentence instead of getting bailed out.

I was fortunate and lucky to have such an amazing support system from my family and friends while I was in prison. I was given money in my account to order items off the commissary list, and it made my stay in the prison a little bit more tolerable. Life is about acceptance, and I accepted the fact that I committed a crime and deserved the punishment that was given to me. Every day in prison was one day closer to living the life that I was meant to live and having a positive impact on so many lives. I woke up happy and optimistic every day in prison. My back and body may have been sore from sleeping on a steel bed with hardly any padding, but that was my current living situation. I accepted it and made the most of it. I would always look forward to the next exciting thing – whether it was a visit from a family member, a friend, getting mail, watching a sports game on tv, or just going outside to get fresh air and feel the warmth from the sunlight on my body.

I experienced much adversity in prison as a former Marine and educated man. I was not the only person in prison with these credentials, nor was I the only person who had ever been in prison with these credentials, but I was definitely a minority. Prison life was a life that was foreign to me. It was dead time, but I realized early on that this was a time to work on myself. I read a lot, listened to music constantly with headphones on, worked out, and wrote a lot. This was my escape from the negative and dreary life of prison. I kept to myself the best that I could, but I was in an environment with 113 other men for about three and a half years of my prison time. We shared a bathroom, showers, and sinks, and we slept in close quarters. It was an eye-opening experience.

Luckily, my mind has erased most of the traumatic events of prison, but from time to time I wake up from a bad dream that I am still incarcerated. One thing that will never leave my mind is the memory of what would happen every time that I had a visit from friends and family. I was strip searched buck naked and forced to bend over and cough. This was to make sure no drugs or contraband were passed to me during my visit and brought into the prison.

I always wanted to speak to others about the terrible, selfish, and immature decision I made on February 5, 2005, that resulted in the most tragic outcome imaginable – a decision and outcome that impacted so many lives in a very negative manner. I started speaking before I was incarcerated, and I knew that was my purpose in life. It first started out as giving back and helping other students make a better decision than I did on that horrific night. I had a counselor in prison that believed in me and knew that I was genuine about sharing my powerful story.

The prison I was incarcerated in, Brooklyn Correctional Institution, was close to my hometown. It was literally less than ten miles from where I grew up, and the prison property bordered the Brooklyn Fairgrounds. I always went to the fair as a kid growing up. This particular prison was filled with over 80% sex offenders, because it was a prison where they would be safer than being in another prison in general population. Believe it or not, there are some morals in prison, and molesting children and women is not a crime looked upon highly by other inmates. However, I was not in prison to judge others; I was in prison for the crime that I committed, and I only worried about myself. There is only one person that judges us in life and that is not me.

Being a Marine and college graduate gave me the mental strength to get through my prison sentence. My first year in prison I worked in the school to help tutor the inmates trying to better themselves to achieve their GED. I loved this opportunity to get out of my prison cell to give back and help others. This also gave me a chance to keep my mind sharp. I spent much of my time reading, writing, and focusing on positive things. I knew that I would not be here forever and every day that passed was one day closer to living the life that I knew I was meant to live. I had so much support from family and friends and loved writing letters to them to keep my mind occupied.

After my sentencing, I was moved to a facility that handled all the assessments of inmates that were sentenced to more than two years and one day to be evaluated and be placed in a prison best suited for their needs. This evaluation included what our medical needs were, what our education levels were, what our level of violence of crimes were, etc. This facility was a maximum level prison, and there were no options to leave our prison cell to go to work and occupy our time. I was in a prison cell for twenty-three hours a day. When I was able to come out, I used the telephone and took a shower for that one hour. We were given food in our prison cells to eat and had no option to go out of our cells to the chow hall to stretch our legs and move around. While being in this maximum level security prison, we were not even allowed to have a lock on our locker that we stored all our belongings in.

My cellmate at this time was serving twenty years for murder and facing an additional fifteen years for another crime of attempted murder. This inmate had no personal belongings and only had what was provided to him by the state. Right from the beginning, I felt resistance from this cellmate, and my intuition was correct. My first Sunday morning at this prison, my dad came to visit me, and I left my cell to go to the visit. I had a great visit with my dad. When I got back to my cell, the correctional officer unlocked my cell door. I opened the door, walked inside the cell, and closed the door behind me. When I turned around, I saw my cellmate writing a letter and eating snacks. I knew he had no paper, envelopes, or snacks when I left and we had not received commissary that morning. This inmate went into my locker and took all my personal items. I had an instant feeling of anger. I spoke up, and my cellmate and I had a heated discussion that nearly turned physical and violent. However, I was able to handle my emotions and think quickly, so I diffused the situation. I told him that I had no problem helping him out and giving him anything that he needed as long as he asked me rather than taking it or stealing it when I was not present. From that moment on, we had respect for one another and played rummy and listened to music to help pass our time in that cell. I knew that this temporary situation of being incarcerated would be difficult, and I had to always be smart and make good decisions, so I could be released as soon as possible.

After my time spent in this maximum level security prison to go through assessment, I was moved to Brooklyn Correctional Institute, where I spent nearly three and a half years of my life. This prison was a big open dorm setting prison where I was in close quarters with 113 other inmates with all different types of crimes committed. I did not know or even care what the other inmates were in prison for, but being there you somehow found out.

While I was at the Brooklyn Correctional Institute, I moved right into the working dorm and began working as a tutor in the school.

Because the crime I was convicted of was considered a violent offense, I was not able to work outside of the prison until my level was lowered. I had to serve nearly two years or more before I was able to work outside of the prison. I accepted that I was not able to work outside and made the most of any opportunity that was given to me to be a model inmate. In my mind, I focused on doing the right thing every day as an inmate. My goal was to have a clean record while in prison so that when the day came to be released, there would be nothing holding me back. I proved myself working in the school tutoring the other inmates working on bettering themselves and achieving their GEDs.

Since I proved myself in this job I was offered the opportunity to be the correctional officer's break room coffee making and cleaning inmate. I would go up to the correctional officer's break room and make fresh coffee, clean up their break room, and take out the trash. I took this job very seriously, and I was grateful to be given the trust to be in this exclusive area. There was a television in the break room, and I was able to check out SportsCenter from time to time and occasionally put on MTV. Most of the correctional officers did not mind me being up there, but there were definitely a few that treated me like the inmate that I was. I will not go into detail about this because that was a time that I like to forget. However, I was extremely happy to be given the opportunity to get out of the dorm that I was living in and to have normal conversations with some of the correctional officers.

I maintained this job until I was cleared for outside clearance. At that point, I worked outside of the prison walls and razor wire fence. I was able to operate a lawnmower to cut the grass and shovel snow during the winter months. This time spent outside was a great break from being trapped inside of the prison walls constantly.

JOURNAL ENTRY FROM PRISON ON January 7, 2011:

"I cannot even begin to express the unbelievable emotions that are running through my body right now. It is about 1:15 a.m. on this very early Saturday morning and it is snowing like crazy outside while I sit on my bed listening to JAM'N 94.5 FM. I found out today around 11:00 a.m. that I would be turning the page on this unthinkable nightmare of being incarcerated and in three plus days I will be leaving this facility to be moved to a halfway house. I am still in shock and my counselor was the person who told me the fantastic news. I knew the day would be coming soon, but it was a total surprise and I did not expect to hear it all today. I am doing my absolute best to keep it a secret in this gossip infested soap opera of a place. This place is definitely not the best environment in the world saturated with very dangerous people. I never imagined being in such a negative and miserable environment ever in my life, but this is my punishment for the tragic nightmare that I have caused. I am the person that is responsible for causing an amazing son, brother, friend, and person to be taken from this Earth far too soon. It is the worst feeling imaginable that goes through my body on a daily basis and I pray every day to have the strength to move forward from this nightmare. I also pray every single day to Rich and all of his family and friends to have peace, healing, and forgiveness in their lives. I would do anything to take back all of the pain that I have caused for so many people."

LIFE AFTER PRISON

To put into words how grateful I am for every little thing in my life does not come easy to me. I cherish every little thing, whether it be an iced coffee or a bag of chips from a convenience store. I appreciate the days I jump into my car with the sunroof open, feeling the sun on my face and listening to the music, knowing that there was a time in my life where I did not have that luxury.

I am grateful for everything in my life. Therefore, I love doing what I do and being able to motivate and inspire other people. This is something I strive to excel at. Life is precious, and I am someone that understands this. One decision can change things in a way that would never be imagined. I am here to remind people of that daily. My decision impacted so many lives in a negative way and still impacts myself and others today. I constantly think about what I can do to be better than I was the day before.

I took responsibility from the moment I woke up from the coma and throughout my trial. I accepted what I had caused, and it helped the healing process between myself and Rich's family. Today we have a relationship, and we can communicate with one another. If I did not take full responsibility and accept my wrongdoing, I would not be where I am today. Rich's family ended up speaking on my behalf at my parole hearing and later ended up writing a letter on my behalf to be granted a complete pardon from the state of Connecticut. This is something I can never repay or thank them enough for. They have given me the opportunity to move forward and keep my head held high. With their forgiveness in their hearts, it allows me to honor Rich and keep Rich's legacy with me.

PARDON LETTERS

Pardon letter written by Randy Bronson:

"I first became aware of Mr. Panus on 2/5/2005, the date of the accident which killed my son, Richard Lee Bronson. I first saw Mr. Panus at trial and became aware of his background as to his service to his country and having no criminal history. I first met Mr. Panus while visiting him in prison. I found Mr. Panus to be very sincere and contrite. I was told by the jail warden and some guards that Mr. Panus was an exemplary prisoner. As police officer and DUI victim I was asked to be the impact speaker at the U.S. Submarine Base in Groton, CT. On two of the occasions I requested that Mr. Panus be brought to the forums and speak along side of me in front of approximately 2,000 Submarine students. Mr. Panus spoke from the heart as to how it feels to be responsible for the death of another person and took full responsibility for his actions. When Mr. Panus came up for parole I was glad to speak on his behalf before the parole board and helped to secure his early release.

Since the time of Mr. Panus' release he has proven my instincts correct by living his life as an inspiration. Mr. Panus has secured employment, married and is starting a family. Mr. Panus continues to publicly speak about his experience hoping to prevent others from making his mistake. Mr. Panus has worked tirelessly fundraising for the non-profit in my son's name, the RLB Memorial Fund Corp. In fact Mr. Panus has become our largest fund raiser. During Mr. Panus' incarceration I told him that when this is all done he needs to move on with his life and become the person he always planned to be. It is with this in mind and his prior mentioned conduct I ask for the complete pardon of Mr. Panus to include all records of this incident. It is from my heart that I believe my son would agree with my decision."

I have always prayed for their forgiveness and every single night before I go to bed, I say the same prayers. What I say and pray for gives me strength and I will continue to do this daily. Without the forgiveness of the Bronson Family, I would not be the person that I am today, and I would not be able to go out and speak to other people and share a powerful message and carry on the honor and legacy of their son Rich, my friend. I have said the same prayer from the first day that I have caused this tragedy and still say the same prayer every night before I go to sleep.

God, please grant everyone that knows Rich and loves Rich and all of his family and friends the healing and the forgiveness in their lives to move forward. God, please grant Mr. and Mrs. Bronson and their son Michael the healing and forgiveness of the loss of their son and brother. Amen. In addition to the forgiveness from Rich's family I also received support from someone that I had no idea how much my story would have impacted his life. This would be the jury foreman from my trial who continued to follow what I was doing in my life inside and outside of prison. His name is Jay Gionet and I would like to share his letter that he wrote to speak at my pardon hearing.

Pardon letter written by Jay Gionet:

"My name is Jay Gionet and I was the Jury Foreman for Michael's trial. I would like to take three minutes to share a different side than what the trial allows me to share in my role as the Jury Foreman. Life is full of choices. I discuss this basic concept with my students and my own children all the time. On a cold winter night leaving after a night of drinking, Michael made a poor choice that changed his life and many others. When I received the notice in the mail informing me that I was selected for Jury Duty, I could have made a choice to opt out using a number of excuses during the initial screening process that would have sent me home at the end of the day. But I made the choice to do my civic duty and continue to be questioned for the jury. I was selected for the jury and had no idea how much it would impact my daily life. I would go to court, but then at the end of the day have to create lesson plans so my students could stay on track. After several weeks we all wished it was over. It was draining in so many ways. We listened to all the facts and kept out the emotion and feelings. When the case was given to us it was tempting to say, "let's get this done and get out of here!" But we all stuck to the oath we took to decide the case based upon the facts. We took many votes and tension built as we could not come to a decision. After the judge sent us back for a final attempt I made the choice to rally the jurors one final time. We sent everyone home to clear our minds. I purchased three sets of colored sticky notes and the next day we broke down every detail we were given. On yellow notes, we wrote down everything we heard about alcohol. On green notes, everything we learned about vehicles, road conditions and the DOT. Finally, on pink notes we wrote down every detail of the timeline. We broke for lunch and came back reading every single sticky note aloud and thinking about how they all fit together. In the end we finally came to an agreement and found Michael guilty based upon the facts presented. After I left that courtroom I could have made the choice to put the events behind me but I chose to use it as a learning experience for my students. I would recount the facts of that night and what

Michael's consequences must have been like in prison, all because of his poor choice on that winter night. I can tell you that as they listened I had most student's right in the palm of my hand and many are impacted by the story. I am confident that Michael has done the same thing sharing this story, trying to prevent another tragedy. This past Sunday I was tired but made the choice to go to church. After church I wanted to head home but I made the choice to listen to my daughters request to go to the bagel store for a breakfast. It was these two choices that put me at a spot where I heard of Michael's pardon hearing scheduled for today. I now had to make a very tough choice to come and support this pardon or look the other way and go on with my life. It would have been easy to say I am too busy, the lessons for my students are more important, and besides who wants to spend their birthday driving 2 hours and sitting in a courtroom. But now that I am not bound by the facts of the case as a member of the jury and can look at the people involved, I think it is time to forgive Michael for what he did. As I mentioned earlier, lives were shattered and never can be changed. But Michael can go forward to live a life where he can impact others faced with the situation that cold winter night. We all make mistakes. We need to pay the consequences and Michael did over the past years in prison. None of us make all the right choices. Today I highlighted some of my good choices but like Michael and others, I have made my share of poor ones. But forgiveness, learning from mistakes, and changing the lives of others is an important part of the process. Now the choice is up to the panel. What choice will you make? I hope that you make the choice to pardon Michael and allow him to move forward with his life."

Pardon letter written by Lt Col Ernest Henderson (ret.):

October 21, 2014

Dear Sir or Madame,

Please accept this letter of recommendation in consideration of Michael Panus' request for pardon. As a retired Lieutenant Colonel in the United States Marine Corps, I have known and been in contact with the former sergeant Panus for thirteen years since working with him in the Marine Corps from 2001-2003. During this time I have come to know him as an honest, trustworthy, and extremely giving person. Sergeant Panus enlisted in the Marine Corps in March 1999 and served this nation selflessly and honorably until August 2003 when he separated to further his education. It was while earning his degree that Sergeant Panus was involved in a fatal motor vehicle accident that killed a close friend of his, and resulted in his conviction of second degree manslaughter with a motor vehicle under the influence of alcohol for which he was sentenced to prison. Subsequent to his accident Sergeant Panus immediately took steps to learn from and move beyond this incident. He finished his baccalaureate degree, then served his prison term as the ideal prisoner - by serving as a role model to others. Though he fully paid his debt to his to society through completion of his sentence, he recognizes that no prison term could pay back the life he took, and he continues to serve as a vocal advocate for DUI driving education. After his parole, Sergeant Panus immediately entered the job market and has been striving to get his life back on course. In doing so he has recently married a wonderful woman who he had grown up with and they are starting a family and expecting their first child any day. Despite all of his efforts to bring his life together, his conviction hangs over his head and is keeping him from reaching his full potential. It has had a detrimental effect on his ability to advance in the job market and consequently has had a negative effect on his earnings. I fully believe the State of Connecticut would be best-served by Sergeant Panus maximizing who he can be by allowing him to compete for employment and advancement without the shackle of a conviction. Through unfettered opportunity, Sergeant Panus will repay this State in dividends as a successful citizen, a family man and the leader in his community that he has the potential and capacity to be. His service to this nation as a United States Marine, his unblemished record both before and subsequent to his conviction, and the actions he has taken to better himself and those around him while he endeavors to be an exemplary citizen bear witness to this potential and support my recommendation for a full pardon. If I can be of any further assistance in this matter. Please do not hesitate to contact me via email or phone.

Very Respectfully,

Ernest H. Henderson II, Lieutenant Colonel, USMC (Retired)

Pardon letter written by Yvette Yarbrough, J.D.:

November 3, 2014

Dear Sir or Ma'am,

I am writing in support of Mr. Michael Panus' application for a pardon. I have known him for over thirteen years as a personal friend. We met in 2001 while mount Michael served as an active duty Marine in my hometown of New Orleans, Louisiana.

I am a licensed attorney in Texas, and I hold an inactive law license in Louisiana. Currently, I am the Executive Director of a licensing and regulatory state agency in Texas. Previously, I served as an Assistant Staff Judge Advocate in the United States Air Force JAG Corps, with my last assignment as the Chief of Military Justice at a mid-sized installation. I am still a member of the Texas Air National Guard and was most recently assigned as the Deputy Staff Judge Advocate for the 136th Airlift Wing at the Naval Air Station - Joint Reserve Base Fort Worth. As a former federal prosecutor, in addition to being Michael's friend, I observed Michael's offenses, trial, incarceration, and release with a unique eye. I have had the opportunity to work with offenders for the past nine years, so I have seen a broad spectrum of responses to such convictions. Unfortunately, many are not able to rehabilitate and turn their lives around the way that Michael has. He is in many ways the model candidate for a pardon. After his release from incarceration, I watched as Michael worked tirelessly to get back on his feet. He worked, attended therapy, spoke at high schools about his offenses in an effort to educate young people of the dangers of drinking and driving, and even organized an annual charity golf tournament benefiting a scholarship fund established by the family of the young man killed in Michael's drunk driving accident. While doing all of these things, Michael always maintained a positive attitude and high moral character. He has never wavered on his responsibility for what happened, and he has always tried to mentor others so that his mistakes would not be repeated. Michael speaks often of

Richard Bronson and the Bronson family, always with a tone of respect and remorse.

Unfortunately, the labels involved with Michael's offenses and conviction have hindered him from attaining his full potential in his employment. A pardon would greatly improve his chances of being able to apply for the caliber of job for which he is qualified. Michael and his wife are expecting their first child any day now, and I know he would like to provide the best life for his daughter that he can. I believe that with a pardon he will be able to do so. I know from personal experience that some view a pardon as a way to erase the past. However, I do not believe that Michael is this type of person. While a pardon will remove the offenses from his record, it will not remove the maturity that Michael gained from going through the process of conviction and incarceration. It will not remove the support system that Michael has in place to help keep him on the path of personal improvement. It will not remove the positive influence that Michael has had and will continue to have on countless young people who have heard him speak and will not remove the remorse that I know Michael feels and expresses for the death of his friend Richard Bronson. The pardon will however allow Michael to attain his full potential in his employment and make the best use of his education. I hope that this board will consider granting a pardon to Michael and respectfully request consideration of such. If the board has any questions or would like more information I can be reached at my email or my telephone number.

Regards,

Yvette T. Yarbrough, J.D.

OVERCOMING ADVERSITY

What is adversity? My definition of adversity is when something in your life becomes tough, difficult, stressful, and not easy. I lost my mother thirty days after being born about six weeks early. The feeling of never knowing your biological mother is a feeling of emptiness and a void. It has been a void that has gotten stronger and stronger as I have gone on longer in my life and become a parent myself. My mother was not there to nurture me, love me, and have that bond that a newborn needed.

You only get one chance at this amazing journey in life, so why do people choose to not live their life to the fullest? Many people fall into a comfortable routine and believe that their life is supposed to be mediocre and that's what life is. I beg to differ; every person has a choice to be the way that they want to be. If you are not completely happy and fulfilled in your life that is your choice. However, you can take steps each day to get your life closer to where you want it to be.

I first started speaking to high school students less than one year after the tragic mistake that I caused in the early hours of February 5, 2005. I contacted my former high school, Plainfield High School and got in touch with the guidance department. They were so supportive, and they wanted me to share my story with the Alternative High School located in Moosup, Connecticut. I was so nervous and excited at the same time. I made a printed out PowerPoint presentation with slides discussing the epidemic of drinking and driving, drinking and driving fatalities, and the horrific tragedy that I had caused. I am not the only one who got behind the wheel after drinking alcohol and became responsible for a life taken from this Earth prematurely – I wanted others to recognize that if they made the wrong choices, it could be them too.

Life is what you make it!! When I was released from prison after nearly four years of my life was put on hold, I entered the work force. I was a thirty-one-year-old, former Marine honorably discharged, but I was also a convicted felon with a bachelor's degree in Business Administration with no business working experience. People that have a clean criminal record have a difficult enough time finding a well-paying job to support themselves.

I have always considered myself a go getter. I started selling night crawlers when I was a teenager to earn extra money. I would do odd jobs such as landscaping, trash removal, stacking wood, and attic clean outs as early as a twelve or thirteen years old to earn extra money. I mainly used that money to buy baseball, basketball, and football cards to fuel my hobby of collecting sports cards.

I first started working at my hometown gym as a front desk attendant while I was in a halfway house after my incarceration. This was the gym where Rich and I always worked out. I became very friendly with the owners of the gym, and they wanted to support me on my transition back into society. They gave me a job there to work the front counter while I was moved to a half-way house in my transition to a law-abiding contributing citizen. This is a very difficult concept to grasp for many inmates who exit prison and are left with no options for jobs. Many inmates leave prison without a college degree, trade, or real work experience. This is the reason why the recidivism rate is so high in many states. Every day when I was in prison, I knew I was left on this Earth for a larger purpose. I did not quite know what that was, but today I do. It is to inspire and motivate people to be the best person that they can be, no matter what happens in their lives.

After working a short time as a front desk clerk at the gym I was offered a position as a dispatcher at a local gravel and excavation company. I was only here for a few short months because I was not up to speed with the required work for this position. I really enjoyed this job because I was making great money, and I was able to operate the backhoe and load trucks with mulch, crushed stone, or processed material. It was just not a perfect fit. I then

94

started working at a local golf course as a groundskeeper. This job was ideal at the time, but the pay was barely minimum wage. It was tedious work, but I enjoyed being outdoors and listening to music on my iPod. After being incarcerated for almost four years and not being able to be outdoors and free, I cherished every second. I have an appreciation for anything and everything that most people cannot comprehend. I had everything in my life and in one second, it was all taken away.

Having acceptance in our lives helps us deal with situations, feel the emotions of that situation, turn the page, and move forward. No matter how small or big the situation is in our lives it causes us to feel emotions. I accepted the fact that I made a terrible and selfish decision on that cold February night that caused the death of my good friend Richard Lee Bronson. There were many variables in that decision for me to choose to drive when I knew I should not have. The possibility of the roads being icy should have made me be much smarter and drive with more caution. The alcohol that I drank that night altered my decision making, judgement, and I made the wrong decision. All I wanted to do was go out and have a great night out with my friends and get everyone home safely. I failed in doing this and impacted so many lives in a negative manner.

I accepted the fact that Rich's family was not ready to speak with me until I was incarcerated. I accepted the fact that I was found guilty by the court of law. I accepted the punishment that was given to me from a judge. I knew that I would be spending five and a half year in prison because of a terrible decision that I made that caused the death of my good friend. I accepted the fact that my life would be on hold for many years and that I would be also serving a five-year probation period. I accepted the fact that I was a convicted felon and my job opportunities would be limited. I worked very hard to become the person that I know I was left on this Earth to be – a person who finds good in any situation and is the best person that I can be. I realized and accepted the fact that I was left on this Earth for a reason. That reason is to become a speaker to motivate and inspire people, showing them that no matter what adversity happens in your life, you can always make good from a terrible situation.

I always tell people that it has not been an easy road, but this is all I know, and life is what you make it. I could have thrown in the towel many times and said my life is over, I spent almost four years in prison, I am a convicted felon, and I will never overcome this tragedy. I am only going to be able to work a job where I can collect a paycheck and have a mediocre life. But no, I instead fought very hard to attain a complete pardon from the State of Connecticut, so I can do the things that every other citizen in the United States of America can do. When I was a convicted felon for nearly eleven years, I could not go hunting with my dad and my best friend, and I could not own a firearm to protect myself and my precious daughter Bella Marie Panus. I am a Marine who served my country; I am not a criminal. I am in no means trying to minimize the tragedy and traumatic result that I caused and the loss of another human life. I made a selfish and terrible decision when I was a senior in college that resulted in a tragedy. However, that one cold wintery morning in February 2005 would not define me as a person. It has only led me to the path that I chose to inspire and motivate people to show strength, determination, humility, gratitude, and perseverance.

I was granted a complete pardon in the year 2016, and my criminal record was completely gone. I could own a firearm and go hunting with my dad and best friend. I could apply for any job that I wanted without checking that dreaded box. Our society labels people no matter what type of person they are. All they want to do is focus on the negative things that people have done in their past. I accepted the fact that I made a terrible decision, and I am making all the right decisions from that day on. I accepted the fact that I married the wrong person and had an incredible child with that woman. Today we focus on being the best parents to Bella as co-parents.

My life is not about collecting a paycheck and just going through the motions in life. I want to have a positive impact on as many lives as possible. I strive to show my daughter Bella that she can achieve anything in her life that she wants to achieve as long as she works as hard as she can. I accepted the fact that I was found guilty of 2nd degree manslaughter with a motor vehicle under the influence of alcohol, and I was sentenced to five and half years in prison. Today I am the BEST daddy there is to my AMAZING little Princess, and I will provide her the best life possible.

DECIDING TO BECOME A SPEAKER

Once I woke up from a coma four days after the tragic accident in the early morning of February 5, 2005, I was informed of the devastation and tragedy that I had caused. My family and friends told me that I was responsible for causing the premature death of my good friend Richard Lee Bronson. Rich was only twenty-three years old and he had just graduated from Eastern Connecticut State University with a degree in Psychology. He was continuing his education to work on his PhD in Psychology. My selfish and reckless decision to get behind the wheel of my car after consuming alcohol was directly related to causing the premature death of Rich.

I went out one night to have a regular Friday night out. I went out to celebrate with my friends, to have fun, to dance, to drink alcohol, and to be a single college student. When I left the bar that very cold early morning on February 5, 2005, the thoughts of being responsible for such an unthinkable tragedy never crossed my mind. My friends and I were so accustomed to going out and having alcoholic drinks and taking turns who would be the driver. I did not make the responsible decision that night to be a designated driver and not consume alcohol. I had the mentality that I was invincible, and I had made it home safely hundreds of times before. Why would this night be any different? That evening and early morning changed my life in many ways; I was responsible for causing the death of my good friend Richard Lee Bronson.

When I woke up from the coma and realized what I had caused, I was heartbroken, lost, confused, and hurt. The life as I knew it before was over. It was a long road to recovery mentally and physically after that tragic early morning. In the beginning I asked myself, "Why me?" Why was I left on this Earth and Rich was not?" It was my responsibility to bring all of my friends home safely that evening, and I failed at doing that. I am the type of person who would never intentionally hurt anyone or cause problems. Living with what I was responsible for is something that I would not wish upon the worst person in the world. I did not know what to do and I was afraid to go out into public and see people. This was a foreign feeling for me, as usually I am very excited to see people and talk to people. I feared what people would think about me now being responsible for such a tragic event. It took a long time to get back on my feet and become a person that was confident enough to go out in public. I received and still receive so much support from the community, my friends, and family – support for which I am extremely grateful. If it was not for all of the support from my family and friends, I would not be the man that I am today. Every single day we are faced with decisions, and every day I work towards becoming a speaker who will have a positive impact on as many lives as possible.

I am a single daddy to the most incredible little Princess, Bella Marie Panus, who is currently four years old. I strive to give her the best life possible while I pursue my passion and purpose as a speaker. Bella calls me a "Magical Speaker" and it melts my heart to know that Bella sees her daddy do what he loves.

I had been working outside sales jobs for larger companies, and it was just not my passion. I first started working for a company called UniFirst, selling heavy soil industrial uniforms and facility service products, such as toilet paper, hand soap, doormats, and carpets. I enjoyed having the flexibility of working outside of an office and meeting with business owners. Sales is a very rewarding career and gives you the opportunity to make a great living. However, working for UniFirst was not fueling my passion, and I was losing drive and motivation. During this time, I had met a former high school classmate of mine and we began to date. We had known each other since we were very young because she lived about two miles from my house that I had grown up in. We rode the bus together, went to school together, and played sports against one another. This person that I am referring to is Bella's mother and I cannot thank her enough for giving me the most incredible little girl in the world. I absolutely love being a daddy to Bella, and Bella gives me the drive, inspiration, and motivation to become the best role model. After getting married, having Bella, working other outside sales jobs, being a stay at home parent, and getting a divorce, I realized that I was meant to be a speaker to talk about the adversity that I have gone through and currently am going through to show everyone how precious life really is.

I speak about events that have happened in my life that have led me to where I am today to become an inspiration to every person that I meet. Being able to approach all situations with a positive mindset has been the way I handle everything in my life. When I learned I was responsible for causing the death of my good friend Richard Bronson, I was in a very low point in my life. I should have never been driving my car while under the influence of alcohol. This was a selfish decision that I had made many, many times in my life since the time that I had gotten my driver's license and starting drinking alcohol. Many people every single day make this same selfish decision and get away with it with no negative consequences. Many people that have a few alcoholic beverages never think that anything tragic will ever happen to them. However, every single time anyone gets behind the wheel of their car after consuming alcohol, they are making a terrible and selfish decision. Unfortunately, as human beings many of us never learn until something painful occurs, and you end up learning the hard way. There is no excuse for anyone to get behind the wheel of their car after consuming alcohol today. There are so many options to get a ride home safely, and it is complete selfishness if anyone decides to drive under the influence of alcohol or drugs. When my terrible decision occurred, I did not have the luxury to use Uber or Lyft to get home safely. But today there is absolutely no reason for anyone to drive under the influence of alcohol or drugs.

(Speaking engagement at Westerly High School, May 17, 2019.
Photo credit, Samantha Robshaw Photography)

FOLLOWING YOUR PASSION AND PURPOSE

Everyone has a place in this world no matter what it is that you decide to do with your life or the career that you choose. I am a 39-year-old divorced dad to a precious little girl, and I decided to become a speaker and an inspiration to every person I meet.

We all have a story, adversity that we face, highs, and lows in life and it is how we react to those things that define us as a person. I never imagined myself being a speaker at military bases, colleges, high schools, middle schools, and being a keynote speaker at larger events when I was going through life. However, this is my passion and purpose, and I will continue to work very hard to become the best speaker possible. I have made many mistakes, but I have also made many good choices in life. Every single day I still learn a lot about myself.

I studied Business Administration in college and listened to other people when deciding what to pursue as a career. I have always been sociable, outgoing, friendly, and positive, so I assumed being in sales would be the best choice for me. I worked in sales for years and had some success, but I was truly missing something. I was not passionate about what I was doing or selling. Establishing friendships and the trust of people and business owners was my greatest quality. However, the product and service that I was selling was not the greatest. Heck, in some cases it was not even average, and I wear my emotions on my sleeve, and I was exhausted mentally and physically. I could not do it anymore.

I made a difficult choice as a single dad to leave my stable paycheck and pursue my passion and purpose as a speaker to inspire other people to follow their dreams. I knew deep down inside that everything would work out and I would give Bella the best life possible while following my passion and purpose. Bella will grow up and see that anything and everything is attainable and achievable if you never give up and work as hard as possible.

Each day we wake up with a new day and a fresh start and the ability to do great things.

I am not telling everyone to give up their full-time job and become a speaker, but I encourage everyone to think very hard about what it is that brings them satisfaction, gratification, and happiness. It may be nearly impossible and difficult at times, but keep working towards your passion and purpose in life. If it means going back to school, getting a certification, furthering your education, whatever it may by, you can do it. If you do not believe in yourself, it will not be possible for you to attain your highest potential and be the best you. In life what other option is there? Going through the motions of life and focusing on things that are out of your control is wasting energy and not allowing yourself to live a full life. Our time on this planet is limited and we only have one shot at making a difference in this world. Be grateful for everything that you have in your life and work as hard as you can to achieve everything that is in your life.

Being able to stand on stage in front of an audience is where I belong to share a very powerful message with them about choices, overcoming adversity, being humble, grateful, demonstrating perseverance, and being determined. One of the points when speaking to my audience involves asking the following question: "How do you respond to unexpected challenges and adversity in your life?" The audience may be full of hundreds or thousands of people, but the question is a personal one because the answer is different for all. The audience is mostly silent, but I tend to zone in on one person that looks to be thinking deeply about the question. Locking eyes with a young adult commonly causes them to redirect their eye contact. We all know the feeling of the teacher calling on you to answer a question. The thoughts can quickly turn into fear of not being prepared, not knowing the answer, or not having the confidence to speak up. Having the gift to provide the confidence to even one person giving an answer when they typically would not speak up is one of my strengths. Having a positive impact on just one person's life and helping them make a better decision than I did is what I consider to be honoring Rich's life.

The feeling that I have when I am done speaking is beyond words and the reason I know I was left on this Earth.

BELLA MARIE PANUS

(Narragansett Seafood Festival, August 2017)

I truly cannot put into words what it means to be a daddy to my incredible little girl, but I will do my best. I was so excited to find out I was having a child. My wife at the time surprised me with a gift bag. Inside of it was a pregnancy test with a positive reading on it. At first, I thought it was a magic marker and I thought to myself, "What am I getting a magic marker for?" I am not too familiar with over the counter pregnancy tests and what they look like, but I realized after a few seconds that my wife and I were expecting a child. We had been married for about six months, and we both were ready to be parents and were trying to get pregnant for a little over a month. When Bella's mother was pregnant, I was excited to become a daddy. I of course was hopeful to have a boy because I love sports, hunting, fishing, and everything else that a daddy wants to do with their son. However, I was just grateful to be expecting a healthy baby. About five or six months into the pregnancy we were able to find out the sex of the baby. As a married couple at the time, we decided to do a gender reveal party at our house to find out the gender of the baby that we were expecting. I will never forget that day for as long as I live, and the look on my face was priceless when we found out that we were expecting a little girl.

(Gender cake reveal, July 2014)

From the first second that I laid eyes on our precious little girl, I instantaneously experienced a love that I will never be able to comprehend. From that first second that I saw Bella's face and eyes, I had tears running down my face. I knew I would love this little girl unconditionally for as long as I live. The love that I have for Bella has only grown stronger as every second, minute, hour, day, week, month, and year has passed by. I cherished the time that I had to hold my little girl, give her bottles, change her diapers, calm her when she was crying, swaddle her tightly, rock her to sleep, and just sit there and stare at the baby monitor as she slept so peacefully.

Being able to spend so much time with Bella while she was an infant is something that I will cherish forever. I decided to be a stay at home dad once Bella's mother went back to work when Bella was four months old. I had recently been granted a complete pardon from the State of Connecticut, but they sent me a letter saying that it would take up to eight months for it to be official so the state could retrieve all the records and documents. At the time my wife and I were living above her grandparents in her mother's house and we did not have a rent or mortgage payment, so me being a stay at home dad worked out with my wife's career. Bella and I were always on the go, whether it was going to the pet store to see all the reptiles, fish, and animals, playing at the park, going to the zoo, visiting the aquarium, hanging out at the beach, playing at the park, and so much more. I am definitely a person that enjoys the warmer weather and living in New England. When the weather is nice, I spend as much time outdoors as possible. I was so excited to have my little Bella with me in everything that I love to do. Bella is my daughter, my best friend, my little princess, and the one person who inspires me to be the best person possible every single day.

Bella certainly cherishes every second spent with her daddy and I feel the same way about every second that I spend with her. Bella and I love being by the water in the warmer months, and we spend much of our time at the beach building sandcastles, splashing in the ocean, and riding the horse carousel at Napatree Beach in Watch Hill, Rhode Island. We also love to visit our friends Danny and Lucy Durand at their lake house on Alexander's Lake to swim, catch fish, take boat rides, kayak rides, and play with their granddaughter who is right around the same age as Bella.

This past year I was the keynote speaker at Cannon Air Force Base in Clovis, New Mexico, and I was able to bring Bella with me on this incredible trip. This was Bella's first time on an airplane at the age of three years old and she was wonderful. I brought her laptop computer with me, armed with a few movies that would keep a very active and energetic three-year-old entertained on the flights. We flew into Amarillo, Texas where we picked up our rental car and headed to our hotel in Clovis, New Mexico. Bella was so well behaved and did so well while traveling. I was so happy to have her with me for this incredible opportunity to speak to the soldiers at Cannon Air Force Base. There was an awesome zoo in town that we visited, and Bella wanted a stuffed animal coyote that she named "Trippy" because it was her first trip on an airplane. Trippy is still one of her favorite stuffed animals to this day. It was Halloween while we were in New Mexico, so I packed her Vampirina costume and I dressed up as Vampirina's Dad, Boris. We went trick or treating with my good friend Sara from high school who had arranged for me to be a speaker at the base. Sara worked on this base and saw that I was a speaker at military bases and thought it would be great to have me come speak to the soldiers on base. I cannot express how grateful that I am to have created so many memories with Bella and what that trip meant to me.

When I grew up my family has always had a garden where we grew fresh fruits and vegetables. Now that I am a single parent to Bella, we are carrying on the same tradition. I have a little spot behind my house now where we plant cucumber and tomato plants. Bella loves to help me plant them, water them, and harvest our fresh fruits and vegetables when they are ready for harvesting.

This shows Bella how to work hard and how your hard work will pay off in the end when harvesting the fruits of your labor.

I am so excited to make Bella's lunch for daycare, draw a handwritten note on a paper towel daily that says "Daddy loves Bella" with four smiley faces because she is four years old. I love picking her up from daycare and having her run up to me with excitement. I pick her up in the air and squeeze her and give her a big kiss. Bella and I have a bond that is incredible. Every single night before I go to bed, I make sure that her blankets are covering her up, and I give her a kiss and I look back at her before I close the door. Seeing her sleep so peacefully makes my heart smile, and I cannot wait to give her the best life possible and be a living example that everything and anything is possible.

Bella definitely has a strong personality. She is very independent, strong willed, extremely funny, and is very outgoing and there is no limit on what her potential will be.

(Napatree Beach Watch Hill RI, September 2016)

FIVE YEAR GOALS

I quit my full-time sales job to become a speaker, finish my book, and put everything into becoming a successful speaker. I am currently driving for Uber during the times that I do not have Bella to make money, pay my bills, and put food on the table. Driving for Uber has not been the most glorious career, but it gives me the flexibility to not miss one second with Bella.

I plan on speaking in every state in the United States of America within the next five years and speak at as many military bases as possible. My overall goal is to have my book issued to every soldier that serves in the military. I want to share a powerful message with every soldier that puts on the uniform to protect this great country.

REFERENCE LETTERS

June 15, 2007

I am writing this letter regarding the case of Michael D. Panus. I knew Richard Bronson since I was in elementary school. We both grew up in the same town and attended the same junior high and high schools, Rich a year behind me. We were both on the same high school football team and both played on the same church sponsored basketball team throughout that time as well. Rich was someone that any community could be proud to call one of their own. While we drifted apart after high school, which seems to often be the case, I still considered Rich a friend and was devastated to learn of his death. After all, we had grown up together and spent most of the formative years of our lives together. I've known Michael Panus for the greater part of the last five years. He is the high school friend of my current roommate and our friendship has grown out of that, to the point where I would easily consider Mike one of my closer friends. Echoing the same sentiment, I had of Rich, Mike is also someone that his community should be proud of.

The morning I learned of Mike's accident, I was sick; I had a friend in ICU in a boyhood friend that I had known for most of my life gone. After the initial anger and dismay subsided, I was encouraged to learn of Mike's wishes to speak at local high schools about what had happened to him. It certainly didn't absolve him of his guilt, but it will help towards preventing future tragedies of similar circumstances. Mike has been vigilant in getting his story out, trying to impart the lesson that drinking, and driving do not mix- something which is extremely important for high school and college age kids to learn. Having the opportunity to vicariously experience this is better than having a fatal accident. This is of paramount importance, especially considering that a high school and college audience consists of kids who are at the age where the prevailing thought is "Something like this could never happen to me." I'm sure Mike thought something like this could never happen to him, and Mike especially would possess the ability to break through that air of invincibility. I wholeheartedly believe that Mike's time would be better spent educating communities about the dangers of drinking and driving than it would be if he were to be behind bars. This is a burden that he himself has to bear for the rest of his life; a burden that must haunt him on a daily basis. To not be able to educate others about this ordeal only compounds the fact that while Rich's life is lost, Mike's would be irrevocably altered. I thank you for your time in reading this.

Respectfully,

Timothy Thompson

June 18, 2007

Have you ever met the kind of person that lights up a room when they walk in? The kind of person people gravitate towards because they just want to be around their amazing spirit? Michael Panus is one of those people. He is so full of life and has so much to offer to this world. If you are having a bad day Mike is the kind of guy who will make you forget your worries just by simply being in his presence. I feel so lucky that I had the privilege of meeting Michael in a college class. I walked into the first day of my Accounting class at Eastern Connecticut State University and took a seat. As I observed the students around me before class begun, I noticed the bored, tired, and "Let's get this over with" expressions on all the student's faces around me. I can remember thinking to myself, "oh Boy, this sure is going to be a long semester!" Then in walks a person I had never seen on campus before. He charged into that room with such charisma and energy. I thought maybe this person had just been having a really great day. He started making conversation with the people around him and cracking jokes with our professor. All of a sudden, I noticed the students attitudes changing. They became intrigued in what he had to say and seemed to be having a fun time in what was originally an incredibly boring class. I was literally in awe with how this one person affected the entire classroom. A few hours later, I went into another Business class and saw Mike chatting away with some of the other students in the classroom. He recognized me from the previous class and introduced himself. Sure enough, Mike impacted this classroom just as he had done in the last. His optimistic outlook on life is something that is very rare to find.

Later that day, I headed to my last Business class. I walked in and was so pleasantly surprised when I saw Mike sitting in one of the seats. I immediately thought to myself, "Yes this is going to be another great class!" From this day on Mike and I are great friends. As the weeks went on, I realized that Mike wasn't just having a great day the first time we met. Every time I saw him, he had this contagious smile on his face. I recall asking him, "Why are you so happy all of the time?" And he responded, "It's just great to be alive!" He is the kind of person that makes you feel that every day is a gift and that life truly is worth living. Quite some time had passed, and Mike and I were continuously in the same classes because of our shared major in Business Administration. One day, Mike did not show up for one of the classes we had together. It was amazing how I was able to notice all of the other student's disappointment when Mike wasn't there that day. He always brought so much energy to the room that we felt like something was missing if he was not there. I immediately called him after class but could not get in touch with him. Days went by and still no word back. People knew Mike and I were great friends, so students and teachers began to come to me asking where he has been. Finally, one day while class was in session a professor got word that Mike was in an accident. My heart dropped. I looked around the room and saw blank, white faces on my classmates. Every single person in that room looked as if one of their own family members were hurt. Our concern for him prevented us from continuing our class. People were working out carpools to visit him in the hospital while others were getting cards for everyone to send to him. Each day we all updated each other about what we've heard on Mike's progress. Every person that ever met Mike was touched by him in such a special way and was so concerned for his well-being. The first time I spoke to Mike after the accident, I was so excited to hear his voice but from the moment I hung up the phone I knew he would never be the same again. I heard the guilt and remorse in his voice. He lives every day of his life with the regret of driving home that night and promised me he would never touch alcohol again for the rest of his life. As time went on, Mike began to turn that regret into passion. He used this negative experience as fuel to express how critical this issue is. He told me that he is going to take full *responsibility for his actions and promised to dedicate the rest of his life to prevent accidents like this from happening again. He is so unbelievably passionate about this that you literally feel it bursting out of him when he speaks. I know how Mike can affect others. I have seen him positively influence so many students in so many ways. Immediately after Mike gave his first presentation at the high school, he called me in pure excitement. He loved feeling like he had impacted these students and vowed to continue to do this as much as humanly possible. Michael Panus is truly an exceptional individual. He lives with the fact that he is responsible for the loss of his good friend. This is a punishment he will face every day for the rest of his life. It does not make sense to keep this person incarcerated when all he wants to do is reach out to his peers. If Mike was given the opportunity, I know he will make a difference in other student's lives. Please give Michael the chance to do what he has always done so well; positively impact others in a way they will never forget.*

Truly yours,

Lisa Manfredonia

SPEAKING ENGAGEMENTS

Speaking Engagements: (Free) - Refers to, not incarcerated. (Inmate) - Refers to, while incarcerated.

November 15, 2005   Plainfield Alternative High School (Free)

May 28, 2008   Killingly Alternative High School (Inmate)

November 4, 2008   Putnam High School (Inmate)

December 10, 2009   Groton Submarine Base (Inmate)

March 19, 2010   Plainfield High School (Inmate)

April 8, 2010   Putnam High School (Inmate)

April 22, 2010   Tourtellotte High School (Inmate)

April 26, 2010   H.H. Ellis Technical School (Inmate)

May 5, 2010   Putnam Alternative High School (Inmate)

May 11, 2010   Griswold High School (Inmate)

May 12, 2010   Killingly High School (Inmate)

May 21, 2010.   Killingly Alternative High School (Inmate)

December 10, 2010   Groton Submarine Base (Inmate)

October 30, 2014   Putnam High School (Free)

November 1, 2016   EASTCONN High School (Free)

February 12, 2017   H.H. Ellis Technical School (Free)

April 10, 2017   The Coast Guard Academy (Free)

July 8, 2017   Summer Stigma Slam 17 (Free)

September 6, 2017   Eastern CT St. University (Free)

October 25, 2017   Grasso Technical High School (Free)

October 27, 2017   Griswold Middle School (Free)

November 10, 2017   Old Saybrook High School (Free)

March 21, 2018   Fort Drum Military Base (Free)

May 21, 2018   Fort Drum, 1 BCT 10th Mnt. Div. (Free)

May 21, 2018   Fort Drum, 1 BCT 10th Mnt. Div. (Free)

June 7, 2018   Plainfield High School (Free)

October 10, 2018   Norwich Free Academy (Free)

October 26, 2018   Cranston West High School (Free)

November 2, 2018   Cannon Air Force Base (Free)

January 28, 2019   Saint Thomas More School (Free)

February 11, 2019   Marianapolis Prepatory School (Free)

March 7, 2019   Veterans Coffee Table Group (Free)

May 7, 2019   Norwich Technical High School (Free)

May 10, 2019   North Branford High School (Free)

May 17, 2019   Westerly High School (Free)

May 23, 2019   Putnam High School (Free)

May 31, 2019   Plainfield High School (Free)

June 14, 2019   Fort Lee High School (Free)